A Walk
Down the Aisle

Also by KATE COHEN

The Neppi Modona Diaries:
Reading Jewish Survival Through My Italian Family

A Walk Down the Aisle

Notes on a Modern Wedding

Kate Cohen

W·W·NORTON & COMPANY

New York   London

Copyright © 2001 by Kate Cohen

For information about permission to reproduce selections from this book,
write to Permissions, W. W. Norton & Company, Inc.,
500 Fifth Avenue, New York, NY 10110

The text of this book is composed in Zapf International Light
with the display set in Zapf International Light with Swash Caps
Composition by Alice Bennett Dates, A. W. Bennett, Inc.
Manufacturing by Quebecor Fairfield
Book design by Jacques Chazaud

Library of Congress Cataloging-in-Publication Data
Cohen, Kate.
A walk down the aisle : notes on a modern wedding / Kate Cohen.
p. cm.
Includes bibliographical references.
ISBN 0-393-04948-5
1. Marriage customs and rites.   2. Weddings—Planning.   I. Title

GT2690.C63 2001
392.5—dc21   00-050044

W. W. Norton & Company, Inc., 500 Fifth Avenue, New York, N.Y. 10110
www. wwnorton.com

W. W. Norton & Company Ltd., 10 Coptic Street, London WC1A 1PU

1 2 3 4 5 6 7 8 9 0

For my husband

Contents

Acknowledgments

From the moment this work could be even loosely described as a book, I relied heavily on the thoughtful responses of my readers: Ralph, Judy, Amy, and Sady Cohen, Jamie Cohen-Cole, Mary Hill Cole, Adam Greenberg, Stephanie Griffin, Melissa Hale-Spencer, Michael Larabee, Caitlin McCarthy, and Terry Osborne. I am especially grateful to Terry, for a reading so thorough I was afraid to look at it (and then glad I did) and to Amy and Adam, for their willingness to talk through the ideas with which I was struggling. I am indebted to Michael, who was a frequent guiding presence on the other end of my phone line; I followed the sound of his voice whenever I felt lost.

Thanks also to the librarians at the Bethlehem Public Library for help with my research, for summoning books from afar, and for providing a peaceful and inspiring environment in which to work. Mary Hill Cole and Elizabeth Greenberg helped sort out my history, and Amy Cohen helped locate Jewish lore and the occasional fact flying about the

Internet. Courtney Bender and Jonathan Dworkin specifically helped me think about vows and religious weddings, and generally inspired me with their lively, opinionated insight. Mary Crittendon showed great and selfless patience with my work schedule, as well as a constant and buoying belief in me.

My agent, Jenny Bent, has been, throughout, supportive, excited, and just tough enough—as well as blessedly efficient and responsive. And, of course, she brought me together with Amy Cherry at Norton. Almost every suggestion Amy made forced me to sharpen my writing and thinking, particularly the ones that made me say, "What?!" when I first read them. It was a great pleasure to work with both her and Jenny.

Finally I want to thank my parents, Ralph and Judy Cohen, and my parents-in-law, Marcia and Lyon Greenberg, for their incredible generosity in giving Adam and me a joyous and beautiful wedding, and in welcoming us to make every element of that wedding mean what we wanted it to.

What Wedding Does:
A Prologue

The spring after Adam and I got married, I lost my wedding ring. I discovered it was gone when I buckled my seatbelt in the backseat of his parents' car; they had picked us up for dinner. As we drove off, I tapped Adam's leg and pointed silently to my bare finger. He raised his eyebrows, but said nothing. Neither of us wanted to make a fuss, to make his parents stop the car. I figured I would find the ring easily enough when we got back. I worked at home; this dinner out was, I calculated, the first time I'd left the house in almost three days. So I knew the ring wasn't resting between books at the library or nestled in the lettuce at the grocery store. It had to be either in the house or on the patch of lawn I had just crossed.

But it wasn't on the floor in the bathroom; it wasn't in the shower drain. It wasn't in the kitchen sink; it wasn't under the pillow I had clutched in my sleep. I looked where I had stood to push my hands into the tight pockets of just-washed jeans, and then I looked all along the floor nearby, where the ring might have rolled. I found a few pennies, some paper-clips, and ample proof that dusting was low on my list of household chores. I found no ring.

It's just a piece of metal, I thought. If I can't find it, I'll simply replace it. We had designed the rings ourselves and had them made on a trip to Italy, but we could have another one made here. It was no big deal. It wasn't as if I'd misplaced my marriage. It wasn't as if I'd lost Adam.

That's what I said to anyone I spoke to the next day, after spending another fruitless hour in search. If I were truly unconcerned, though, I wouldn't have mentioned that I'd lost the ring in the first place. Instead, "I've lost my wedding ring" became my answer to the question, "How are you?" As the days passed, I got more and more anxious; I alternated between despairing of the search and searching in less and less likely places—taking the sheets off the bed, sifting through the flour bin, emptying the contents of the filing cabinet.

It wasn't fair. I shouldn't have lost my ring; Adam should have lost *his*. Neither of us had worn a ring before we married. And for the early months after we married, Adam couldn't stop playing with his, placing it on its edge on the coffee table and flicking it to see how long he could keep it spinning. I had fiddled with mine some at first too, sliding it on and off absently, turning it over in my fingers, but I had gotten used to it by then. My ring finger, which had felt clunky and encumbered when the ring first went on, now felt thin and naked without it.

It wasn't in the bottom of the garbage can in the kitchen; it wasn't in the grimy nook between the toilet and the bathroom sink; it wasn't in the toe of any shoe in my closet. Could I have baked it into a loaf of bread? I glanced at the freezer, considered thawing and pawing through the recent stash. I considered renting a metal detector—the kind people use to comb the beach. Or hiring a hypnotist to coax the ring's whereabouts from my subconscious. But no, I told myself, if I find it, I find it, and if I don't, who cares? It's just a symbol of my marriage with Adam; it's not the marriage itself.

At brunch with my friend Lissa, six days after I had lost my ring, I shrugged and said I figured that the ring was gone for good. And I tried to make myself believe I didn't mind. But Lissa was upset about the loss and refused on my behalf to give up on the ring: she announced that she was coming over later to find it. I told her not to bother, that I had looked already, that she shouldn't trouble herself over a little piece of metal. But she was unbudgeable, and I was, secretly, relieved.

When Lissa arrived with her husband that night, I was in the kitchen getting dinner ready, trying to act as if this were a social gathering rather than a search party. But Lissa didn't want to eat until the ring was found. So we all four went outside to scour the lawn and the gravel drive until it got dark. At which point, discouraged, I said, "This is silly; I'm going to boil the pasta." While the water heated, Adam and Gary went to search the living room one more time, and Lissa took our vacuum cleaner bag outside to rummage through the cat hair and the dust; I could hear her sneezing as I made the salad dressing.

Oh, no. I'd forgotten—her allergies. I should have stopped her when I saw her with that bag. She wouldn't have let me, though, I knew; she wouldn't give up until the ring was found, or at least until she was satisfied that there was nowhere else to look. If she hadn't had kids to go home to, I would have taken her literally when she said she was not leaving till we found it. Lissa is devoted to her friends; she is also passionate about love and everything connected to it. She believes fiercely in the importance of the wedding ring, in the importance of the wedding. She saw the loss of my wedding ring as tragic. Her wedding day twenty years earlier still loomed large and vivid in her memory; she saw it as a turning point in her life. To her, that's what all weddings were.

Through the screen door I could see her back hunched over as she hunted. There I was pretending I didn't care whether we found the ring or not, when really I cared so much I could hardly concentrate on anything else. Tearing lettuce and slicing cucumbers were about the most complicated tasks my worried brain could handle, and I tore and sliced with extra force—ripped and chopped—as I silently scolded myself. At first I hadn't thought losing the ring mattered, but gradually I had begun to realize it did. It mattered a lot. Yet I refused to let myself get upset—while letting my friend, eyes itching and throat swelling, panic for me. Why did I have to pretend not to care?

I had gone through roughly the same process with the wedding itself.

Before we wed, I hadn't seen our wedding as important or momentous. I had thought that it, like the ring, was just a symbol: meaningless on its own, it meant something only because of the love for which it stood. When Adam and I decided to marry, we had been a couple for seven years. We'd been living together, had made a home together. Our life was routine; our money was merged. Our families even thought of each other as family—my mother took his sister to dinner in Paris; his brother went to my sister's house in San Francisco for a Passover seder. We had long planned to spend the rest of our lives together, married or not. So wedding, I had thought at first, would just symbolize that coupleness, officially declare a commitment that had long existed. Our wedding couldn't be a turning point in our lives as Lissa's had been in hers. It might *say* something, but it certainly wouldn't *do* anything—wouldn't change anything about our lives.

Since the statement was all that was left to make when we wed—our home and lives together having been made already—we planned extra carefully what our wedding would say. What it could say that would be true. Could we make promises to each other when we couldn't predict the future? And would we imply thereby that we had found a perfect love—could we say that we were truly meant for each other?

Married friends told us that even though we were living together already, everything would change when we got married. Just wait and see, they said. I said, Right. I'll be waiting. Our lives were so intertwined already that only four people on our invitation list were unknown to one or the other of us: Adam hadn't met one set of my parents' friends; I hadn't met one set of his father's first cousins. I said, How could marrying so long after making a home together make any sort of difference? And yet, as our wedding date neared, I began to wonder whether it might. Crafting a true statement about ourselves hadn't been as easy, as automatic, as I thought it would be. Trying to make a symbol that really stood for us forced us to think about what "us" was. So I found myself believing that our wedding could mean something after all. Hoping that it could. And if it could, if marrying could mean something for modern American live-together couples like Adam and me, what then should we make of the modern American divorce rate? Did the strong statistical chance that our marriage would fail take that meaning away again?

Even though the odds were that any marriage had a good chance of failing, and even though our marriage—our life together—had begun long before we would walk down the aisle, the closer we got to the wedding day, the more it seemed that wedding did mean something. People argue the opposite. People argue that being able to live together before the wedding, and being able to divorce so easily after it, have rendered the modern marriage meaningless. But the more we thought about our wedding, the closer we got to it, the more I disagreed. Now that couples have to choose to wed (since it's simple enough just to move in together), now that it's so easy to divorce, marrying and being married mean more, not less. Saying something when you don't have to, making a public promise when you don't have to, keeping that promise when you don't have to *is* doing something.

It did something for us. In making that public statement, in wedding, we went through a ritual that nine out of ten Americans go through at some point in their lives. So in wedding we joined the community at large more fully than we ever had before, more fully than we'd ever expected to. We also gathered together for the first and only time the smaller community of the people we loved. We brought it together to show our gratitude for its blessings, and to take our place in it, officially, as adults.

Just wait and see, those married couples had said knowingly, it will all change. And after we married I had said, triumphantly, Nope. We're just like we were before, only with rings on our fingers and with more stuff in the china cabinet. But that was a lie. It was true in a technical way: our everyday lives were exactly the same as they had been before we were husband and wife. Being married really didn't change anything. But *getting* married had. Making that public statement—figuring out what to say, and to whom, even deciding to say something publicly at all, deciding that, indeed, our community had a stake in our relationship—had changed not our daily lives so much as our understanding of our daily lives. Wedding had changed our relationship to the world.

I hadn't expressed such a thought even to myself, even nine

months later, but I knew intuitively that our walk down the aisle had changed us. So when I told people now that it hadn't, that our wedding was just a symbol, I did it out of a combination of habit and pretense. Maybe it was a habit and a pretense I should drop. Maybe I should admit that wedding had done something, can do something; maybe I should think through what wedding does. Because "just a symbol" sounded false to my ears now; it was something I had believed before we wed, before I learned that symbols could not just say, but do.

I was draining the linguine when I heard a shout from the living room. Adam came in and took my left hand off the pasta pot, and slid the ring onto my finger. He and Gary called Lissa inside to tell her—they had, they explained, taken all the cushions off the couch, turned it upside down, and shook. It was a sofabed; the ring had tumbled from somewhere deep within the frame. I hugged Adam, I hugged Gary, I hugged Lissa. Then I hugged Lissa, I hugged Gary, I hugged Adam. I managed to toss the pasta with the pesto, but then I had to put down the wooden spoons to clutch my ring and give four or five little hops of joy. Grinning, I brought the bowl to the table, placed it in the center, and hopped some more. It was just a piece of metal. Hop, hop. And now it was back where it belonged.

A Walk
Down the Aisle

1
With This Ring

If you had been distracted in the backseat, and you'd heard the tone but not the words, you'd have thought Adam and I were eagerly agreeing to stop for lunch at the next exit. In fact, we were agreeing to get married. No diamond ring, no memorized speech, no declaration of love, no trembling "Will you marry me?"

We were on the way home from the wedding of a childhood friend of mine. I had lost and regained touch with Courtney a couple of times over the years; each time we reconnected, we had to work to get past small talk and awkwardness. It was an effort to regain our old intimacy, but we still believed it was there, and that it mattered. Our childhood friendship was vital to our memories of ourselves as children. Her attic bedroom, "my" chair at her family's kitchen table, the dank stone cellar where settlers were supposed to have hidden from Indians—these were as much the landscape of my childhood as my own house. Maybe I hadn't seen Courtney in a while, but I could still hear her practicing the piano, could still smell the paint in the stairwell where I had sat to listen, could still smell *her*. Adam was surprised that we received a wedding invitation from a woman he had never met, but I wasn't.

I'm not quite sure what it was about Courtney's wedding that spurred us on. For me it might have started when I spoke to her about a month before she got married. I asked her about her wedding vows. Adam and I were at the phase in our lives when we were attending four or five weddings a year, and the words each bride and groom chose to speak to each other fascinated me. I had high hopes for Courtney and Jonathan's vows. Theirs was a modern American wedding, the kind that came after living together, the kind that would occur not in their parents' home town, but in the city they shared as a couple, the kind in which every decision on every point was up for debate—not predetermined by society or religion. There was no single society or religion to predetermine it, anyway: Courtney was Virginia Mennonite and Jonathan was New York Jewish. Their common world was an intellectual one: he a scientist, she a social scientist, both were poised to enter the highest circle of academe. They would marry at Rockefeller University in a ceremony performed by a Methodist minister, a friend of Jonathan's family. In other words, it would be a modern intellectual intermarriage under academic auspices. Never was a couple more likely to write their own vows.

But when I asked Courtney whether they were indeed going to write them, she laughed. "Oh, that never works," she said. "Homemade vows are awful." They were going to use the vows in the Book of Common Prayer, the ones we all know by heart, no matter what our religious affiliation: "I, (bride), take thee, (groom), to my wedded husband, to have and to hold from this day forward, for better for worse, for richer for poorer, in sickness and in health, to love, cherish, and to obey, till death do us part. . . . With this Ring I thee wed, with my body I thee worship, and with all my worldly goods I thee endow." These words were written in the mid-1500s, a response by the Church of England to a popular desire for a prayer book in English instead of Latin. Some version of them can be heard at most Protestant weddings, in most movies representing Protestant weddings, and even in the phrasing and rhythm of many vows the bride and groom *think* they made up. They are the standard vows, as far from writing one's own as you can get. But that was the point, Courtney told me. She and Jonathan figured that these words—famous, four-hundred-year-old phrases with the ring of matrimony—would carry collective rather than individual meaning. Exchanging such vows would symbolize their union rather than attempt to explain or define it, which had to be better than trying (and, she implied, failing) to put their feelings into words.

"Really?" I said, and felt a bit naïve when I added softly, "Well, I think we'll probably give it a shot at ours." There it was, magically materialized: "ours." Our wedding was at this point more an assumption than a plan. We'd been a couple for seven years, lived together for most of those, and had made a home for the past four in part of an old farmhouse on the land Adam farmed in Albany, New York. We were happy and settled and we intended to marry one day. I, at least, had begun to think of our wedding as an actual event. And speak of it that way, too, if only long-distance to an old friend like Courtney. The long distance may have been the crucial element: Adam's and my families were eagerly awaiting the Big Event; for years we had been deflecting their hints and questions with a forcefield of shrugs and vague smiles. But on the phone with Courtney, who had no contact with our families, it was safe enough to let the event acquire a reality. Suddenly, "our wedding" existed.

Courtney radiated an almost illegal happiness throughout her wedding, which was small and low-key and felt very real. There are weddings where you feel at the end as if nothing really happened, as if all the elements were assembled, but no reaction took place. And then there are weddings where you can see and smell the chemical change as it occurs, where you know you are witnessing a moment of transcendence. Courtney's was that kind of wedding. It was also a wedding full of good conversations with strangers, a wedding at which one could sit down with the bride and groom and talk, not just coo at them as they made the rounds. Adam liked Courtney right away, and, though before the wedding he had been baffled by her invitation, *at* the wedding he was touched that she had wanted me to be there. Among the guests, there was a jumble of cousins from the valley in Virginia where we grew up, and an entire faculty of Swarthmore and Princeton friends, but I seemed to be the only unrelated guest from her childhood. I think this made Adam, who is sentimental about his own childhood friends, want to tie the knot—not ours, perhaps, so much as his with them. He wanted to make a similar gesture of enduring love for *his* loved ones: he wanted to make a guest list, pick a wedding party, count out the treasures of his life, past and present. And, too, there was something about their small, quiet wedding that made wedding seem so manageable. So, driving home the next day, in a buzz of intense back-and-forth revelation and agreement, an excited conversational high we hadn't ridden in a long while, we talked about wedding. We talked of ceremonies and receptions, of whose weddings we'd admired, of how we could ensure that the chemical reaction that makes a wedding feel like a wedding would take place at ours. "Ours"— there it was again. By the time we turned into our gravel drive, we had decided we would marry on the Sunday of Labor Day weekend, August 31, 1997.

Our wedding was going to be in Virginia. This we'd settled on after years of intermittent bickering. But now that the question was real and consequential; we returned to it with a new urgency. Now it became an argument. I live in Albany, I told Adam, I live where you grew up. I want to get married where I grew up. Yes, it's true all my friends now, save Courtney and a couple of others, are from Albany, or at least from somewhere in the Northeast. But it's also true that those friends have never seen my childhood home, never seen where I came from. My parents have been to your childhood home time after time, I said to Adam. When am I ever going to get your parents to mine except for this?

That was the fair part of my argument. The unfair part had to do with whose parents gave better parties, which father would try to control the event more, and so on. Adam tried half-heartedly to accuse me of being sexist: when it suits me, he said, I argue the bride's prerogative. That was the unfair part of his argument. The fair part was that I was going to be in Italy from January through May, helping my father run a foreign study program, and that it would be much simpler, given the time restriction and the distance, to plan an Albany wedding.

Arguments look so logical when they're written out this way. When you can't see eyes rolling in ridicule, when you can't hear voices sharp with sarcasm. When the two sides are shorn of loaded terms, underlying issues, long-held resentments. As I said, we had long ago decided the wedding— whenever it happened—would be in Virginia. A return to that question should have prompted, at most, a brief logistical discussion and some teasing. But this was a fight, because it was really about other issues. Adam didn't want me to go to Italy; he thought I was either trying to please my father despite my own desires or, if I really wanted to go, being irresponsible about work and unrealistic about how hard it is to plan a wedding. I felt ambivalent about going, but I wanted to travel, and felt I had the right, almost the obligation, to accept an offer to live in Florence. After all, Adam was more than welcome to come too.

I knew he wouldn't. Beneath his anger at me was his frustration at the slow start of his construction business and his need to feel settled in a career other than farming before turning thirty and before marrying, two milestones he would reach within the year. Go ahead and go, he said. He wouldn't even promise to come visit. I will go, I said, and I won't feel guilty about doing something you could do with me if you'd just let yourself.

But I did feel guilty. That was my issue beneath the issue beneath the argument, my unspoken feeling. And he was going to miss me. That was his.

I wept angrily and he seethed woundedly and I didn't want to touch him and he didn't want to speak to me. And still the wedding was going to be in Virginia.

My parents started to search for a wedding site, under the threat that we would put off matrimony another year if they didn't find a place before my father and I left for Italy. It had been seven years already; my parents took their mission seriously. We had daily phone updates, and in the mail within the week a sheaf of carefully numbered photographs and a list of corresponding explanations. See, I said to Adam, look how organized they are, how diligent. The perfect wedding-helpful parents. They found a place and we agreed to it, pleased: it was a museum of frontier culture, which featured five working farms. We would marry in what looked, from the outside, like a dairy barn, and dance in a rough-hewn octagonal barn. Understated, whimsical, not a wedding factory, not a country club. We assigned the band search to my younger sister and her boyfriend, the caterer search to a family friend, and I made a few calls in search of a rabbi. See, I said to Adam, this isn't so hard. Then I went to Italy.

Adam and I don't have many arguments. We have small bouts of bickering, intense expressions of irritation that, we both know, rarely have anything to do with the putative subject of the bicker. If Adam comes into the kitchen while I am trying to salvage a cake I have broken, chances are our interaction will be hostile; I will be frustrated and angry with myself and annoyed to be caught mid-blunder, and I will take issue with whatever issues from his mouth. His only hope would be to say nothing, but neither of us is good at that. Likewise, if he comes inside scowling and oily from a bout with a recalcitrant tractor, any question I ask—from the state of the machine to what movie he wants to see that night—will fill him with fury.

Real, substantive arguments, on the other hand, seldom occur. When they do, they are even more seldom resolved. Perhaps because we are both competitive in argument and unwilling to cede points, we rarely end disputes with a compromise or a decision. Neither of us ever says, "I'm sorry, I was wrong, let's do it your way." Or even, "You know, that's a good point." Or even, "Look, since we can't agree . . ." Since we can't say these makeup words, we never actually make up. We simply resume our lives. Perhaps that is a resolution of sorts, not in the sense of coming to a single point of agreement, but in the older sense of the word, from *resolvere*, to loosen and dissolve, to "change or convert by disintegration." Our opinions and desires, knotted and hardened into fact and necessity when we argue, unravel and relax with time. They melt, thaw, and resolve themselves into a dew. We cannot integrate our disparate beliefs into a single course of action; instead, our rigidity, our intransigence, *dis*integrates.

And yet we aren't back where we started from, either. There's something alchemical in that process of melting and hardening and melting. When the rhythm of our daily lives solidifies once more, we feel stronger as a couple. Maybe, whether we can admit it or not, we understand each other better. Maybe it's the simple transaction of trust and need and urgency that underlies a painful fight: you don't lose your cool, you don't bare your feelings, you don't *care* so much with anyone but the one you love. Most of our arguments have to do with feeling secure about each other—at that moment before Italy, it was, Are you going to leave me at regular intervals throughout our marriage? and Are you always going to refuse to share my adventures?—so arguing desperately, intimately with each other, trusting each other with our fears and our ugliness, helps soothe the very insecurity the argument expresses. It's a mysterious process, the forging of union through contention, the resolving of crisis into calm.

Adam did come to visit me in Italy. I was living in an apartment in Florence with my father; my younger sister, Sady, a student in the college program Daddy was running, also was in town. Adam and I had been emailing daily: he relaying discussions he was having with my mom (still in Virginia) about wedding minutiae; I proposing, among other things, that when we were in Florence together, we would try to write our vows. I felt we needed to get an early start on the essential part, the part that makes it a wedding rather than a party: the public vow. And, after having been apart for a while, missing Adam, and feeling that strange sense of closeness to him that we have after we fight, I wanted to express what I felt about him, to put our love, our life, into words.

A few days after he arrived, we tried. Though we had enough privacy to talk about it in the apartment, we didn't sit down to write our vows at the kitchen table. We invested the project with a sense of ceremony. I packed paper and pens, and we trudged up a snaking series of streets to Fort Belvedere, where you can sit on the ramparts in the sun and look out over the city of Florence. We didn't talk about our vows on the walk; we waited until we were settled on the smooth stone surface, with the bare paper in front of us. And then we looked at each other. Well? And there was much contemplative kicking of the wall, and much gazing out at the rich red tiles of the Florentine roofs, and a little embarrassment. I jotted down some notes: "family," "trust," "one life." Kicked the wall, looked at the city, tried to eavesdrop on some passing teenagers. We didn't get much further than that, didn't even venture into the realm of the sentence. The right tone was almost impossible to find: we wanted to avoid sounding too legal, too pragmatic, too political, too poetic, and too unrealistic. We couldn't say life was a river, or love was a journey, or marriage was the union of two hearts. But we wanted to say more than that we were good friends who pledged to brew a comforting cup of tea should the need arise.

The tone wasn't the only thing that was difficult; the content, too, was elusive, even troubling. What could two people promise each other? Could they promise to make each other happy? I recently came across the wedding vows used for Jack and Jennifer's wedding on *Days of Our Lives*. They said, "Now we will feel no rain / For each of us will be shelter to each other. / And now we will feel no cold / For each of us will be warmth to each other. / Now there is no loneliness." The idea that life would now be eternally warm and dry and companionate because Adam and I were marrying seemed about as farfetched as, well, a soap opera. That sort of thing exists only in a world where the bride and groom are clearly meant for each other because their first names begin with the same letter.

We weren't always going to be happy or feel safe. We were certain to be lonely once in a while. But, happy ever after or not, could we promise to stay with each other always? That's the central thesis of many traditional vows: "till death do us part"; "as long as we both shall live"; "all the days of my life"; "throughout all of our days." Could we swear that one of those nasty arguments about nothing and everything would never, rather than disintegrate our differences as they had so far, simply disintegrate *us*? Could we vow that death instead would be the thing to part us?

Some people get around the forever issue by promising to do what they've pretty much done so far: stay together while they make each other happy, love each other as long as they can. "As long as we both shall love," so to speak. But that seemed less a promise than a statement of the obvious; as long as I'm happy, I'll be there, you can count on me. Could we swear to stay if times got bad, that was the question, if we found ourselves one night years from now staying up late, he in the living room, I at the kitchen table, waiting for each other to go to bed first, putting off that moment that we'd have to retire to the same bed and listen to the space-filling sound of someone we no longer loved breathing too close?

We didn't think this would happen to us, but we had turned our backs to each other in bed just often enough to be able to imagine it. We didn't think it would happen to us, but people were divorcing all the time who didn't think it would happen to them, who believed—who had promised—they would stay in good times and in bad. Could we honestly vow we would hold on no matter what the future held?

If not, could we promise at least that we'd be good to one

another, and leave aside the question of forever? Our friends
Mike and Caitlin had the year before promised to love, honor,
and trust each other "as we live our lives together," not stip-
ulating how long that life together might be. They promised
also to support each other as they grew and changed. But
what if the change is for the worse? People promise to be for
their spouse "a refuge of love and strength," to listen and
comfort one another. I hoped I could do that, but I was
doubtful. Never slip up? Always be kind and loving and
"there" for one another? Simply staying together seemed easier than that. Well, should we promise to *try*? Or wasn't that
enough?

We had lived together a long time, and now we were getting married. The thing that turned living together into marriage was the vow. And since we were writing our own, since
we were free to make whatever promises we wanted, the
burden on us was even greater to make them promises we
could keep, but also promises worth making.

So we were at an impasse, getting chilly in the growing cool
of the evening. We watched silently as the sun set over the
skyline; its beauty, in light of our failure to write something
beautiful—to write anything—now seemed more daunting
than inspiring.

Down in the streets a few days later, Florence was beautiful
still, but dirty, beautiful but bedraggled, beautiful but rough
with human life: the shouts of neighbor to neighbor, the
imprecations of the vendors at the market, the always shocking, always too close roar of the moped. Adam and I decided
that, though we couldn't make our vows come out properly
yet, we could at least shop for our wedding rings. Florence is,
after all, a city of jewelers. The glinting old bridge that arches
over the Arno is lined with jewelry stores, their shop windows

awash in gold and silver. Surely the perfect ring was out there, waiting to be discovered. But we soon learned that it wasn't, that in Italy a wedding ring is just a wedding ring: gold, rounded, slim, with little variation. The jewelry equivalent of the Book of Common Prayer, it was, apparently, what all marrying Italians exchanged. We wanted something a little different, something slightly unusual. We felt *we* were slightly unusual, I guess, and couldn't imagine having exactly the same ring that everyone else had. I knew how to say *heavy* in Italian and I quickly learned the words for *flat* and *matte*, and we trudged from shop to shop, finding nothing we loved, but learning a bit about gold. Such as the fact that less perfect gold, less luxurious gold, makes a better ring. "Eighteen carat is better than twenty-two for a wedding band," said one jeweler, in a shop between the Ponte Vecchio and the Pitti Palace. "It's stronger. Remember," he winked, "it's supposed to last a while."

Jewelers like to work with gold; it has great malleability and tensile strength, which means they can do almost anything with it. They can also melt it and harden it over and over without shattering it, and thus rework it endlessly. In fact, though the gold this jeweler was working may have come from South Africa, where over half the world's gold is mined, or from North America, Australia, or even Italy, it may just as likely have come from old jewelry. Gold never rusts, tarnishes, or corrodes, so throughout history, very little of the stuff has been lost. It just gets melted down and made into something else. Your wedding ring could well be made from someone else's ring, from some other age.

Gold has been the traditional material of choice for wedding bands since about the second century C.E. Before that, the ring might have been made of braided rushes or grasses, then of carved ivory or amber, then of iron or copper. But gold was all the Florentines were now selling in their black velvet cases of *anelli nuziali*, and the qualities we ascribe to gold—purity, preciousness, luster, solidity—have become attached to the symbolism of the wedding band.

Gold also symbolizes, even stands for, money. From ancient through medieval times, wedding bands resounded with the clink of the coin. They were given not at the wedding ceremony but upon betrothal, from the groom to the bride, as a sort of down payment on the wife to be purchased, as proof that a groom could afford to take a wife, or (the most romantic of the mercantile interpretations) as a symbol of his bride's share in his worldly goods. For this last purpose, the ring would have a key attached or a signet engraved, power to open a man's storehouses or sign his name. All of these early rings were *pledges*, both in the sense of deposit or collateral, and in the sense of promise or vow. In fact the old English word for pledge is *wed*; the wedding ring was the *pledging* ring.

If the association with gold had its more practical, less romantic side, so did the shape of the ring. Some have called it a descendant of the slave chain, or of ropes with which prehistoric man bound his chosen mate to claim ownership. Samuel Johnson, in his 1755 *Dictionary of the English Language*, defined *ring* as "a circular instrument placed upon the noses of hogs and the fingers of women to restrain them and bring them into subjugation." Enforced or not, this union was meant to be binding, and the ring frequently stands as a symbol of that bond. Rings are part of most Western ceremonies today, and many Eastern ones, but even ceremonies without ring exchanges *per se* often include strings of beads, garlands of flowers, or cords of silk with which the wedding officiant might join the hands—and bind the lives—of bride and groom.

The ring also symbolizes eternity. This may seem like a more modern metaphor than the slave chain, but in fact it dates back to the Egyptians. Since then, designs on wedding rings have come and gone, from hearts to joined hands to interlocking vines, but it is that perfect round, with no beginning and no end, that persists as the ultimate symbol of enduring love.

Over the years, the wedding band came to be used as the crux of the wedding ceremony rather than as a pledge to marry (engagement rings took over the earlier function). Jewish weddings once occurred in two distinct ceremonies; the first was betrothal, which included the ring, and the second, which could be months or years later, was the nuptial ceremony under the wedding canopy. But in the eleventh century, those two parts merged into one. Similarly, for English-speaking Christians, the double-ring wedding ceremony, in which both bride and groom exchange rings as part of the ritual of becoming man and wife, was codified in the sixteenth-century Book of Common Prayer. With this shift, the clink of the coin and the rattle of the slave chain quieted, so that what the ring came to express, what it came to symbolize, was the wedding vows themselves. The marriage itself.

Which is why that jocular jeweler advised us to buy the stronger kind of gold.

Unfortunately, his advice was more intriguing than the rings he was selling. Or the rings anyone was selling. So Adam and I, after two days of looking, decided to have the rings made. A new friend, an American painter living in Florence, was taking jewelry-making classes; she said she would introduce us to one of her teachers, a woman named Pao. We made an appointment for late one afternoon, and, street address and street map in hand, found Pao at work. I was disappointed immediately. My fantasy image of a Florentine jeweler was a twinkly-eyed man or woman hunched over a polished wooden table, the wise and witty master of a tiny, unpretentious shop on a side street in the Oltr'Arno.

Pao was young, Taiwanese, and mistress of a metal desk in one corner of a large, fluorescent-lit, backpack-strewn studio near the Central Market. She did not wax philosophical about love and marriage; she did not, in fact, say anything. Her English was so-so, but her Italian was good; the problem seemed to be cultural, not linguistic. Adam and I discussed the design in front of her, leaving pauses for her to jump in with her expert opinion, and she never jumped. She just smiled timidly at us, unless asked a direct and unambiguous question.

This might have worked if we knew exactly what we wanted, but we didn't. Neither of us could draw; neither of us had ever worn a ring of any kind. We had talked some about a design, but flat and matte and heavy were all we had decided on. We liked the silver look of white gold, so . . . white gold, I guess. As for a pattern . . . out came a pen and the notebook that carried our failed attempts at vow writing. Well, how about sort of a diamond pattern, like this, running through the center, but with plain and polished edges? Pao assented. She didn't say, "Oh, that will be lovely, and lovelier still if we add this element here . . ." She just said she could do what we asked, then she measured our fingers and gave us a price and a date for the fitting. We walked out forty-five minutes after we'd come in. As I stepped onto the pavement outside her studio, the misgivings I'd suppressed in the presence of others seemed to bubble up my throat—this is too fast, too fast, I thought. I'm going to be wearing this for fifty years, and we just made it up in less than an hour? And the pattern was completely arbitrary: a struggled, tense compromise between Adam's desire to have a symbolic pattern and my desire to have none at all, it was a visual joke (the diamond ring I'd never otherwise own) that happened to look nice. We stopped at a café for a drink, and when Adam went in to order, I started to cry. It takes me twice the recommended time to choose cheap shoes I'll own five years if I'm lucky—why did I think we could make up in a moment a wedding band, a meaningful, beautiful wedding band we would love forever?

Adam calmed me down by offering to cancel the commission; certainly it wasn't too late. We decided, though, after much discussion, not to phone Pao to call the whole thing off. That was as positive as our decision felt at the time: simply not ending a process that felt scarred with disappointment and uncertainty. I didn't press to cancel the commission because I didn't want to be someone who would back out of an agreement and because I worried about what my new painter friend would think of me. The rest of our interaction with Pao was an anxiety of vacillation, miscommunication, and financial dispute. She had miscalculated the cost of the gold and had to raise the price of the rings; we felt misled and uncomfortable, but we felt even worse after telling her that. We changed the design, removing the diamond pattern that didn't seem to mean much, leaving a kind of etched (or "Florentined") center, but then wondered whether our rings would have any real distinction.

When I went to pick up the finished rings at the end of May—Adam had already gone back to Albany; our vows were still unwritten—I was looking forward simply to the end of the ordeal. Pao met me on the steps of Santa Croce; I had planned to take the rings into its Pazzi chapel afterward, to try to invest them with some of the calm and spirituality of the place. But when the moment came, I forgot my plan entirely. Smiling with shy pride, Pao handed me our rings in a little scarlet velvet purse, with "lui" and "lei" (his and hers) embossed in gold over each pocket. I was shocked when I saw them: they were, in fact, beautiful. Forged from bickering and indecision and all the messiness of money and ignorance, they were little glistening pieces of perfection. And they fit.

A few days later, in early May, Courtney and Jonathan came to Florence on a delayed honeymoon. It was right before my return home, and the waning days of my stay, oppressively hot, were frantic with shopping and cleaning and packing and saying goodbye. The three of us spent a few moments of peace together, hands wrapped around cold drinks at an outdoor table at Caffè Ricci, near Santo Spirito. I told them about Adam's and my brief attempts to write our wedding vows; I told them I now understood why they had chosen not to. There's so much pressure to get them just right, to make promises you can keep, but promises worth keeping. They told me that, if you take them seriously, the tried-and-true vows can be difficult too: Jonathan said that he had had trouble with the promises spelled out in the Book of Common Prayer. He felt odd, he said, swearing that he'd be there through thick and thin when he didn't really know what thin was like. His parents had never had marital problems, and he and Courtney had never had much stress in their relationship. So far, everything had been good; how did he know he would be capable of sticking around if things got bad?

So he ended up making a public promise, a promise to the woman he loved, that he wasn't sure he could keep. But maybe that's what you have to do. Maybe you don't have to be certain to make promises; maybe in marrying, you make the leap from what you are sure of and know about yourself to what you hope to be true of yourself. And maybe by making the leap you make it true—or at least, more true. Maybe it was like our rings: you had to pull out a notebook, put something down on paper, and believe that it will be right.

Even if you're not designing your own, you have to have faith that the rings you choose today will still be right in fifty years. You don't have to know for sure.

In the mid-1600s, long after the double-ring ceremony had become official wedding ritual, the English poet Robert Herrick wrote:

> Julia, I bring
> To thee this ring
> Made for thy finger fit;
> To show by this
> That our love is
> (Or should be) like to it.

In those last two lines, Herrick tosses in between parentheses the essential problem: "is / (Or should be)." There's a big difference between "is" and "should be"; everyone's relationship *should be* not too constricting and not too loose, as the poem goes on to say, and as endless and "as pure as gold." But what if it isn't? What does the ring mean if "Or should be" is as far as you can honestly say? Their love might not be perfect, but still Herrick gives Julia a symbol of perfection. In his poem, the ring becomes, for two people trying to have the love they should, a kind of compass or map: this is what we're aiming for, this solidity, this perfection. A daunting example to follow, yes, but maybe less so when you remember that a ring might be melted and hardened over and over to make it beautiful, and that the design might be argued over and changed and changed again. That it too requires work before it's perfect.

I took out that scarlet pouch about twenty times in the days before I left Florence, showed the rings repeatedly to people who had most likely been satisfied by their first look. I couldn't believe how lovely they were, how perfect. Our love, our marriage might never be that perfect; we didn't know. But we could still make promises to one another. Vows have to do not with present perfection but with future hopes; they push a wedding (a *pledging*, remember) into the conditional "should." Everything else about the ritual—the dress, the tuxes, the music, the flowers—implies that all is perfect as it is today, as perfect as it gets. The happiest day of our lives. Everything else about a wedding says "is," but the vows tell the truth, the vows say, not yet. They are like the poem that Herrick gives along with his ring. They say "should be," hope to be, try to be, want to be.

2
Love Song

> BOSWELL. 'Pray, Sir, do you not suppose that there
> are fifty women in the world, with any one of
> whom a man may be as happy, as with any one
> woman in particular.'
> JOHNSON. 'Ay, Sir, fifty thousand.'
> BOSWELL. 'Then, Sir, you are not of opinion with
> some who imagine that certain men and certain
> women are made for each other; and that they can-
> not be happy if they miss their counterparts.'
> JOHNSON. 'To be sure not, Sir. I believe marriages
> would in general be as happy, and often more
> so, if they were all made by the Lord Chancellor,
> upon a due consideration of characters and cir-
> cumstances, without the parties having any choice
> in the matter.'
>
> —JAMES BOSWELL, *The Life of Samuel Johnson*

Before Adam left Florence, we went to shop for wedding dress fabric at Casa dei Tessuti, a venerable fabric store a block from the Duomo. My elderly cousin Rachel, who lives only a few blocks from the store, sent her live-in companion, Aurora, with us, but excused herself on account of the cold. She did, however, phone ahead from her apartment to make sure we would be well received. I did not have enough of a sense of Florentine society and my cousin's place in it to know whether the Signor Romano she spoke to was try-ing hard to remember her name, or making a face on the other end of the line—Here we go again with Signora Neppi

Modona—or preparing to welcome us with the utmost ser-
vility and the lowest prices. So we set off hesitantly, warning
both Aurora and Rachel that we weren't necessarily going to
buy anything.

Casa dei Tessuti, on the inside, looked like a library in a
country house: wooden shelving, wooden floors, warm light,
brass fixtures glowing gently. Like a well-used, beloved library,
it had a kind of cluttered opulence: fabric was stacked, bolt
upon bolt, floor to ceiling—silks and satins and fine wools of
every imaginable color, weight, and texture. Walking into
Casa dei Tessuti, we stepped into a world where everything
could be lovely and well made, where the lowliest pair of scis-
sors would sit heavy in your hand and crisply cut carefully
measured cloth.

Signor Romano and his brother, Signor Romolo, were im-
peccable. Their clothing seemed grown on them, as soft and
lustrous as human skin—just shirt, sweater, tie, and suit, but
somehow you couldn't imagine them in department store
clothes. You couldn't imagine them in anything factory-
made. Signor Romano gave us his steady, patient attention.
He was in his sixties, physically graceful and efficient as he
pulled down bolt after bolt of silk and unfurled the fabric
with voluptuous ease across a wooden table. He told me that
for my skin tone I must have white white, not off white; he
listened, head cocked, as I described my imagined dress. A
friend at home, the woman who had made my prom dress
and my sister's wedding dress, had agreed to turn whatever
material I chose into a simple gown, with a fitted top and a
flowing skirt. She and I had spoken of a nice, soft, brushed
cotton. Signor Romano and I picked silk crêpe de Chine.
Rather, he picked it and I agreed, reluctantly; I wasn't certain that something so luxurious belonged on my body, but
this store, this man, made one feel that luxury was the way
it was supposed to be. Not a sin, not a sign of weakness or

greed, but a hymn to God. Manmade fibers, stiff fabric, anything poorly wrought was an error, an insult, a waste of our precious time on earth. Yes, that snowy white silk crêpe de Chine would be just right.

And then we looked at lace.

Adam had insisted on lace. In flipping through fat Italian bridal magazines, I had been drawn to the simplest possible wedding dresses: one lovely fabric, graceful neckline, *basta*—enough. "It looks like a nightgown," Adam would say, when I showed him. "What about this one?" he would point. And "this one" would have pearls or sequins or lace, like a wedding dress. I am not a frilly person; the simpler, the more beautiful is how I see things; aesthetically speaking, I would have made a good Shaker. But I was pleased that Adam cared what my dress would look like, and I was determined to honor his image of our wedding, just as I expected him to honor mine. Lace was the only frill I could stomach—at least it was cloth, not craft supplies. So I agreed that we would have some lace.

It was all kept in a large box, the kind you might use for storing letters at the top of your closet. The first piece of lace Signor Romano spread out in front of us was the most elegant I had ever seen; it looked like a gauzy field across which someone had scattered flowers. Very free, very modern, he said, with an expressive flutter of his hand. Beautiful, I breathed. Aurora loved it too. Adam said he wanted to see what else was there. Ah, said Signor Romano, you are lucky not to be the first Adam, who had to take what he was offered. You can choose any woman in the world, and you chose this one. And therefore you should choose your lace from all the possible lace.

You have to choose also what kind of love you want, said Signor Romano, as he started to sift through the box. There are two kinds, he said: "amore," the love of Dante and

Beatrice, an eternal love of light and intellect, a spiritual love; and "love," which is about physical attraction, pleasure, and comfort—the body, not the soul. He pulled out another piece of lace, much more traditional-looking, much more heavily worked, and placed it next to the first. Wait, he said, I have something I want to show you.

He went into a back room and returned with a poem he'd written on a visit to Yosemite, "Velo di Sposa" ("Bridal Veil").

Dov'è il nero cratere	Where is the black crater
che partorì la bianca	that gave birth to the white
montagna.	mountain,
Il ghiacciaio che la scolpì.	The glacier that carved it,
L'argento dei fiumi	The silver of the rivers
che la imprigionarono.	that imprisoned it?
Millenni oscuri ammanta	Forest moss cloaks
il muschio della foresta.	the dark millennia.
Soli due alberi	Only two trees
stretti in tenero abbraccio.	bound in a tender embrace.
Bianca cascata	White cascade
sull'alto dirupo	on the high precipice
è velo di sposa	is a bridal veil
mosso da giovani venti.	moved by young winds.

This he softly, dramatically intoned, and then roughly translated for Adam. Here I translate literally, losing the music of the Italian, the import of it, the care with which Signor Romano smoothed out the paper and signed the bottom "To Ketty & Adamo, with best wishes . . . AMORE!" Clearly Signor Romano was in favor of otherworldly, spiritual love.

It seemed an odd moment to haggle over price, and so, perhaps seeing that we were spellbound, our guardian stepped in. Aurora (tough, protective): "Do well by them, Signore, remember, they are young, they don't have much . . ." Romano (sly, charming): "You get married only once, you know . . ." With either lace, the material would add up to $350, more than I had wanted to spend on a finished dress. We went home to consider it. I had intended for it to be a nice dress, but I believed it was wasteful to spend a lot on something I would wear only once, and $350 would be more than twice what I had ever spent on a dress.

People used to get married simply in their very best clothes; there was no such thing as a wedding dress per se. If she could afford it, the bride might buy or make a new dress for the occasion, but it would certainly be a dress she would wear again. The wedding dress as we know it in the West seems to be a product of the industrial revolution; the more-or-less simultaneous rise of the middle class, consumer society, and mass communication; and the romanticization of marriage for love. It all came together at Queen Victoria's wedding in 1840. The newspapers and ladies' magazines that proliferated in the nineteenth century trumpeted the event and described her dress (and the entire ceremony) in the intricate detail we have come to expect from fashion reporting. Driven by steam, the textile industry began to mass-produce affordable fabrics, and a new gadget called the sewing machine (invented in 1846) brought the fashion industry a much wider public. A public that, apparently, wanted to look like the Queen.

So the British middle class copied Queen Victoria, and we Americans copied them, and that's why, when we think of a wedding dress, the first image that comes to mind is pure Victorian: full, long sleeves, train, floor-length hoop skirt, head covering. Later in the century, the skirts straightened and the bustle appeared—because that's what was happening in fashion in general, and wedding dresses were still simply a lavish version of the fashion of the day. Which also meant that women still usually remade or altered their wedding dresses for future use. White was a popular color (it was what the Queen had worn), but it was not the only color; difficult to keep clean, it had a limited life for reuse. More than purity, white symbolized affluence in the nineteenth century; poorer women had to choose more practical colors.

But bridal gowns gradually parted ways with current fashion, as bridal fashion became a distinct subset of the fashion industry. One historian traces the shift to the 1930s; *Bride's* magazine was first issued in 1936. Certainly wedding dress fashion continued to be affected by general fashion trends, but it was no longer determined by them. In 1971, for instance, when minidresses were the rage, 87 percent of wedding dresses were floor-length. Today's wedding dresses often sport Victorian touches, such as a train, that would never appear on our best dresses in normal life. That's in part because the bridal industry encourages women *not* to think of their wedding day as normal life. It promotes the idea of a once-in-a-lifetime event, one day, one dress, one true love. Accordingly, we are expected to buy one very expensive wedding dress in wear-once white, a dress cut in such a way that no one could mistake it for a regular dress; then, after we are wed, put it in an acid-free box in the attic, and hope, maybe, that our daughters will share our taste and waist size. Wedding dresses today are likely to be the most expensive dresses we ever buy and the only dress we have made to suit us.

I know $350 sounds like a paltry sum to anyone in the market for a dress to wear on the Happiest Day of Her Life, but the thing is, I didn't believe in the Happiest Day. And I didn't believe that I was somehow destined to have a certain dress any more than I believed I had been destined to meet a certain man, that I had a single, predetermined soulmate. Adam and I were well suited, loved each other, had made a happy home together. But Adam, however wonderful, wasn't the only man in the world for me, and this wasn't the only cloth.

But I couldn't shake the spell of *amore* that Signor Romano had cast. Some part of me yearned for the fairy tale, no matter how much I denied it, no matter how clearly my real life countered the fairy-tale conceit. (Nowhere in the story does it say that Cinderella lived with Prince Charming for a while at the castle before setting a date.) A week later Adam and I returned to Casa dei Tessuti at dusk, and I bought the silk and the lace with the scattered flowers. I bought, if only for the moment, the idea of spiritual union; I bought the idea that Adam had chosen me among all women, that we were two trees bound in a tender embrace, alone except for one another, fated to be together. I bought the white cascade. We lingered in the store as long as we could with Signor Romano and his brother, for an hour after they had closed the doors to other customers. They wrapped our crêpe de Chine and our French lace as tenderly as if they were wrapping *amore* itself. And Adam and I walked home carrying this package between us just as the setting sun was gilding the buildings that lined our way.

At our dining-room table back at the apartment, we opened our precious packages to show the silk and lace to my father and sister. It must have put visions of the Happiest Day in their heads because later, cloth carefully rewrapped and table spread instead with dinner, they pressed to know what our first song would be. Adam and I demurred: they would find out when the band played it. We weren't being coy; we simply had no idea what our first song would be. We hadn't thought about it much till then; we would end up debating the question all summer long. It mattered to us because, like every other aspect of the wedding, every other decision that we made, we felt it said something about who we were. At first, we thought about not having a "first song" at all:

though we enjoyed being the center of attention, having everyone watch as we looked deep into one another's eyes for a solid three minutes or more seemed a bit much. But we planned to hire a band for our wedding, and we knew that at some point after dinner the band would start to play. There would, we imagined, be a *de facto* first song; everyone would just wait to dance until we started. So we might as well choose what we would be dancing to. We flirted with and then rejected irony and humor—"Stand By Your Man"; "She's No Lady She's My Wife"—figuring that though we might look back later and regret a joke, we would not regret an attempt at sincerity.

There was one song we loved, one song we thought sounded and said something right: Lyle Lovett's "Nobody Knows Me." It has a simple, plaintive tone, and describes in few words the lived-in quality of our kind of love. The narrator describes the little things about him—how he likes his coffee, what he eats for breakfast, that he likes to sleep late on Sundays—and his refrain is that "Nobody knows me like my babe." We called each other "babe" too, when no one was around. But "Nobody Knows Me" is, if you listen closely, a breakup song; in the end, after recounting obliquely a fight about an affair, the narrator declares that he hates to be alone on Sundays. I didn't think we could use a breakup song, however subtle, however much we loved it. Adam argued that no one would actually be listening to the words, but I knew I would.

I suggested "Like A Rose," a Lucinda Williams song I had played over and over on my tiny college stereo around the time Adam and I started seeing each other. It's another simple song, more about falling in love than being there already: "Everything we have is fresh and new, / I will open myself up to you like a rose." That song, just with the opening chords of the guitar, could pluck me back into that moment in college right between being alone and being with Adam. But the truth was, everything we had *wasn't* fresh and new, and we kind of liked that fact. "Like A Rose" was not a marrying song; it was a courting song.

Adam argued for "Stewart's Coat" by Ricki Lee Jones. It was beautiful and sad-sounding, but I couldn't make out the words. Even the lovely chorus—"I'll see you through it all, just give me time to learn to crawl"—we weren't entirely sure of. "Crawl" rhymed and made sense, but we could have sworn she sings "grow." It seemed risky to commit to a "theme" song when we couldn't make out its theme.

None of these songs would be played at our wedding. We chose "What A Wonderful World," a song that doesn't try to characterize love at all (and therefore couldn't mischaracterize ours), but which instead celebrates how it feels to be in love: "I see skies of blue and clouds of white / The bright blessed day and the dark sacred night . . ." But "Nobody Knows Me," "Like A Rose," and "Stewart's Coat" were all included on a tape Adam made that summer. It was an idea we came up with in Florence, when my sister and father were tossing out song titles for our consideration. We asked our friends and family to tell us which love songs they loved; from their suggestions, and all the ones we added to them, Adam made a two-cassette compilation to play during the wedding weekend: Love Songs.

The love that these love songs describe divides pretty cleanly into two categories: eternal love and earthbound love. Or, as Signor Romano would have said, *amore* and *love*. In eternal love songs, people fall in love instantly, when they first glimpse one another. "The First Time Ever I Saw Your Face" is an eternal love song, as is "Love Walked In." Because that's what love does in these songs, it just walks through the door, recognizable, undeniable, and usually in the form of a perfect person—a person to whom you could say without irony,

for instance, "You're The Top," or whom you could con-
ceivably compare, sweetness-wise, to "Tupelo Honey." Since
"Every Little Thing She Does Is Magic," such a person, bringing with her such an immediate, overwhelming, "Crazy
Love," changes everything. Eternal love makes you happy
where once you were sad. It makes what was once murky
and confusing in life bracingly clear. And it does so forever;
eternal love songs describe a love that not even death can
diminish, a love that continues for all time. In eternal love
songs, "Love Is Here To Stay," and not just for the night. In
that particular Gershwin tune, love outlasts both modern
telecommunication and a mountain range. Unusually brazen,
perhaps, but not an unusual sentiment for eternal love songs:
in all of the songs that celebrate *amore*, love lasts till the end
of time; they never even hint at finity.

Earthbound love songs express a different kind of love. In
these songs, love rarely just walks in; you either have to go
chasing after it, or it has to be "Strong Enough" to break
down your door. If it does walk in easily, it's because you
can't recognize it for what it is; the love in these songs often
begins in friendship, in antagonism, or in courting so full of
conflict you're tempted to say, "Let's Call The Whole Thing
Off." Once you're finally in earthbound love, once you finally
admit to yourself that "It Must Be Love," your life is better
than it was before (these are still love songs, after all), but
only incrementally so. Life is still hard; the person you love
just helps get you through it. She drives for you when you're
too tired or drunk; she hands you a glass of water when
you're thirsty; she calms you down. She makes you feel
good—not perfect, not free from care, not as if life suddenly
had meaning. Just good. And the good feeling you get from
earthbound love is bound by time and place: she looks
"Wonderful Tonight," for instance, in "Our House." What
will tomorrow bring? What would happen to your love if you

were suddenly transported somewhere else, if the nest of specific daily ritual were disturbed? Who knows? For here and now, it's good, say these earthbound love songs, and that's worth something. Worth enough even to work at; in eternal love songs, love is a state of being, and once you're in, you're in. Earthbound love songs often imply, on the other hand, that love requires effort, concentration, will.

The three songs that we considered for our first dance and then cast aside were about earthbound love, love that eats breakfast, love that has to be coaxed, love that needs time to learn to crawl (or grow). I guess that's because we felt we had an earthbound love, that making any claims toward the eternal kind was a bit presumptuous, if not dishonest. We couldn't say we had been shot with Cupid's arrow; we did not fall in love at first sight. I met Adam one evening when I was a sophomore in college and he was in his junior year (since he had taken two years off, he was twenty-two; I was nineteen). He was the friend of a new friend, Carol. She and I had planned to go out to dinner to get to know one another, but when she picked me up one evening in mid-October, she told me that she wanted to stop for someone first. So we drove to Adam's apartment about a mile from campus, though I would have preferred not to share my new friend on our first evening together. But I had little choice in the matter; Carol, I later understood, was setting us up. I cringe a little when I picture Adam and me then; we were both wearing hats at the time; I wore a rotation of black felt hats from wide-brimmed to bowler; he wore a single brown Australian rancher's hat. Not exactly standard headgear at Harry's Truck Stop, where we went for dinner.

I could tell you who sat where and at what booth; the evening made an impression on me. The company, specifically, made an impression on me, because though I could tell you where we were sitting, I have no idea what we ate. But love, instant and undeniable? No. Adam spoke and carried himself unlike any college student I knew; he seemed calm, sure of himself, but without any need to impress. I liked him. I liked them both. A week or so later, I went with Carol to his birthday party, and after that I spent more and more time with them and their friends. I couldn't say when I first went out with Adam alone, but I do remember thinking about him more and more, to the point that, finally, I couldn't even study one day. Studying defined me in college; I was shaken not to be able to do it. So I called Adam and asked him to meet me, and when he did I told him that I was perfectly happy in my independence and wasn't looking for a relationship at all. In other words, I told him I wasn't going simply to let him walk right in the door. OK, he said, fine. He didn't believe me, though, and shouldn't have; it was as if I'd opened the door and said, "I'm absolutely not going to notice that you're there."

At home for Thanksgiving break, I talked about Adam a suspicious amount, and someone finally asked me if something serious was going on between me and this Adam. I dodged the question, but I thrilled to hear the name "Adam" come out of someone else's mouth; I came back to school a day early to surprise him. He answered the door in his bathrobe; he was watching a football game. I remember sitting next to him on the couch and feeling his body heat through the flannel.

It was a slow process, in other words—I can't even begin a new paragraph after body-heat-through-the-flannel with "That's when I knew I was in love." Because it wasn't. And not just because I was happy enough on my own and hesitant to risk falling in love, but because we did not instantly see in one another's faces "the one" that eternal love songs promise us. We didn't see blessed perfection, the moon and the stars and the sun all rolled up into one. We saw a possibility, one among many. At that birthday party, the second time I met Adam, he was interested in me, but he was interested in two other women as well, a vivacious jazz singer his age, and a sexy older friend of some friends. I, meanwhile, would soon be confused about my interest in Adam because a friend I'd had a crush on for a year was recently single again. We had a choice, in other words. As Signor Romano later pointed out, Adam was not the first Adam; he did not have to take what he was offered. Note, however, that when Signor Romano told Adam he could choose from among all possible women, so he should get to choose from among all possible lace, he didn't just hand Adam his box of lace samples; he offered him a choice of precisely two. Adam's choice of women and my choice of men were limited by time and circumstance. But it was still a choice.

Dante was the lover in Signor Romano's mind when he spoke of *amore*. Dante's *La Vita Nuova*, a hymn to his beloved Beatrice, is an eternal love song; in it, love hits Dante instantly, on page one, when he is nine years old: "The moment I saw her I say in all truth that the vital spirit, which dwells in the inmost depths of the heart, began to tremble. . . . From then on indeed Love ruled over my soul." The object of his love, Beatrice, is incomparable, divine even: "She is the sum of nature's universe. / To her perfection all of beauty tends."

Immediately, irreparably, without any sense of free will or choice, Dante is in love. Unlike the first Adam, my Adam didn't have to take what he was offered, but also unlike the first Adam—and unlike the lovestruck Dante—he didn't have an ideal mate divinely created just for him. Nor did I. We had choice, but not certainty. Without having God hand us our mate, without getting struck by the arrow, the light, the lightning bolt of eternal love, how do we know we've found *the one?* How do we know this is the one we should wed, the one with whom we should try to make a marriage?

I don't think we did find *the one* that night at Harry's Truck Stop. At that point in my life, seven and a half years before we chose the lace for my wedding dress, I could have chosen many another man with whom to make a happy life. I chose Adam because he was sturdy with integrity, bright with intelligence, thoughtful, funny, good. At that moment, I could have chosen someone else; Adam and I were not destined for one another. The psychoanalyst Erich Fromm writes that love in contemporary Western culture "is supposed to be the outcome of a spontaneous, emotional reaction, of suddenly being gripped by an irresistible feeling." As Dante was. We didn't have that when we met. Our love was "essentially an act of will," which is how Fromm describes love in arranged marriages. "It is a decision, it is a judgment, it is a promise. If love were only a feeling there would be no basis for the promise to love each other forever."

The decision, the judgment, the promise—they were all there. But the spontaneous, emotional reaction was there too, now. Somehow, when I looked at Adam in the months before we married, I saw not a present and future act of will, not one of many men, but *the one.* I had that irresistible feeling.

At the time we met, we were just another mismatched earthbound couple; he said potato and I said potahto. Now, nobody knew me like my babe. Not just what I liked in my coffee, but how I folded my socks, what I would say about a movie as soon as it ended, whose letter on the kitchen table would fill me with dread. We had learned each other's worlds, too: he knew now—and he didn't when we met— what dolmades were, what Giotto did that no one had done before, the difference between *fewer* and *less.* I knew now—

and I didn't when we met—what a joist was, what constituted a suicide squeeze, the difference between disinvesting and divesting from South Africa. We hadn't begun with the eternal-love sense of being made for each another; through sheer accumulated knowledge, we became made for each other.

I knew, without asking, that Adam would be waiting for me in baggage claim when I flew back to Albany at the beginning of June. He knew how keyed up I would be, that I would be thirsty but not hungry, that I would call my parents before I went to bed. Which is why, when we looked at each other under the wedding canopy three months later, we wouldn't be thinking, well, you could just as well be someone else. We would feel the lightning bolt instead. As if by magic, we would each find ourselves standing next to our one true love. As if by magic, but not by magic at all. We weren't destined for one another when we first met. Over the years, we had destined ourselves for one another.

Marrying is about more than finding—or making—the love of your life. It's about more than the moment of lightning, of realization. It's about forever, too. If we can destine ourselves for each other, if we can, by dint of effort, make of ourselves the eternal lovers for whom we were searching, could we make the forever part too? Could we make the years that stretched ahead stretch "to the end of time"? Isn't that, more than whether there's a certain someone out there just for you, the question that those earthbound love songs implicitly ask? Whether eternity is possible? Yes, those songs sing of a love that begins gradually and bumpily, rather than smoothly all at once, but how they really differ from their eternal cousins is in their attitude toward permanence: they grasp today and now, not willing or not able to touch forever.

And yet, in a sense, they are willing, they are able. I shouldn't, in fact, be calling them "earthbound love songs"; they are songs about earthbound love, but the songs themselves aren't earthbound at all; the songs themselves *are* eternal. Writing a song about a moment when you tell your wife she looks wonderful, or even a moment when you ask her for a glass of water, lifts those moments into another realm, makes them transcend their own insistent temporality.

The way, say, making a swath of fabric, whether it's cotton or silk, into a wedding dress lifts it out of the mundane, pulls it toward the heavenly. The way wearing your best dress on your wedding day makes it a wedding dress. The way marrying—stopping the rush of time long enough to consecrate our love before our loved ones—would pull our earthbound love, almost against our will, toward the eternal.

3

Beginning in the Middle

In mid-June we started getting presents—for our engagement and from distant relatives who knew they wouldn't be able to make it to the main event. I was grateful for the crystal vase or the damask tablecloth, but I couldn't help thinking that these presents were going to the wrong person. The custom of giving housewares to a marrying couple seemed attached to a different kind of wife, the traditional kind, the kind who becomes a new person, with a new name, when she marries. As a new person, about to start her new life in a new home, she is utterly without serving pieces. She is a naked newborn thing; she must be given sheets and towels and cash, she must be accoutered ("she" and not "he" because she, in this same tradition, is the one who keeps house). But I didn't feel new or needy; I had a hefty collection of housewares. I felt I was posing, as I sliced through that packing tape, as a young bride-to-be.

My mother had been a young bride. She was twenty-one when she married, as was her groom. All she had been called upon to furnish so far in her life had been her dorm room. When she married, she had no tablecloths, no candlesticks, no vases—she had no plates. Or sheets or towels or mixing bowls. She had Doris Day and Judy Collins records, the works of Antoine de Saint-Exupéry, posters from Dartmouth's Winter Carnival. She had her clothes: bell-bottom jeans, skirts to change into when it was time for dinner, minidresses she wore to greet my father on his weekend visits to Wellesley.

Adam and I would marry thirty summers after my parents did; their anniversary was in mid-June. I paused in the midst of wedding planning to talk to my sisters about what to give them as a present, what our parents could possibly need thirty years after beginning their lives together. It was hard to imagine the sparceness at the start of my parents' marriage; their house was now a clutter of accumulated stuff. They were trying to reimagine it, though, return a bit to the beginning: after my wedding, they planned to sell the home my sisters and I had grown up in. They were going to build their dream house.

When I mentioned my upcoming wedding that summer to anyone I didn't know well, they asked me, "Where will you live after you get married?" To me it was a funny question, on the order of, What will you wear after you get married? or What food will you be eating as a wife? Why should this aspect of our lives change? I didn't say we were moving, I said we were *marrying*. We had, after all, made a nice home together for the past four and a half years in a roomy farmhouse. Our phone number was the one among the three daughters that everyone in my family knew by heart—the other two were still moving too often. Sure, some day we would build our dream house, too (or, let's be honest, Adam would, while I quibbled over paint color), but it wasn't exactly on our list of things to do that summer.

"Where will you live after you get married?" I realized, was a question from my parents' era. Though they had known each other for almost three years when they wed, the longest stretch of time they had spent in one another's company before their wedding was four days, a long weekend in New York City. After their honeymoon, immediately following their wedding in Atlanta (which immediately followed their college graduations), they moved to Durham, North Carolina, where my father was to begin a Ph.D. program in English. Where my parents, in other words, were to begin their life together. My mother had no middle name: her birth name slipped conveniently into the middle spot to make room for her husband's last name, now hers as well. On formal occasions and on envelopes she became Mrs. Ralph A. Cohen. She was starting a new life. "Where will you live?" comes from a time when that's what a wedding meant—not a new legal status or a new level of commitment, but a new life.

A look through the wedding pages of the *New York Times* the day my parents were married, June 18, 1967, compared to those of August 31, 1997, the day Adam and I were married, shows how different weddings were then. The first thing you notice is that it's exhausting to read all the announcements—there were more than fifty, versus the twenty-some on the day we were married. There's another sign that weddings were generally more important in 1967 than thirty years later: they were announced at the end of the first section then, rather than at the end of the ninth section as they are today. Today they follow close behind the hemlines and society news, in the "Style" section. But when my parents married, if you started on page one with "China Announces It Has Exploded a Hydrogen Bomb" and "196 Vietcong Killed in Ambush of GIs," and you kept turning pages, you would eventually come upon "Sally Dodge Becomes Bride of Michael Mole."

Weddings were, symbolically at least, real news items in 1967, not fluff, and the bride was the lead topic: almost all the photographs accompanying the wedding articles are of a bride in a veil, alone. One veiled bride stands next to a groom; one bride, standing alone, has no veil. Other than those, there were only photo after photo of smiling female with head covering. As for the rest of her costume, it was, in all of the longer articles (about half of the total) described in detail: "The bride wore a gown of ivory peau de soie with long sleeves and square neckline, and a veil of heirloom lace"; "The bride wore a gown of embroidered organdy with a tulle veil and carried gardenias." I couldn't find a single description of a bridal gown in 1997's announcements, except in "Vows," the chatty, boxed wedding feature by Lois Smith Brady (a column that did not appear in the 1967 wedding pages). More grooms (and no veils) appeared in photographs in 1997, but there were still plenty of photographs of brides alone. No grooms alone, of course. Picture that: a page of men in tuxes, some grinning, some glamorous. It's unimaginable, even in the new millennium; brides are still the stars of the wedding.

Something else hasn't changed that much either: the women seemed, then as now, to be headed toward careers. Not as many as are today, but many more than I had expected, were working or about to work, in advertising, at the telephone company, as travel agents, social workers, editors. The big difference is that their mothers hadn't. Over and over, the fathers' professions are given, and the grandfathers', but no mothers', no grandmothers'. These women of 1967 were in the first wave, it seemed. And indeed, thirty years later, in the announcements of their daughters' and sons' weddings, there they are in the background, with careers: "The bride, 29, . . . is a nurse working in a pediatric practice in New York . . . Her mother is the staff supervisor for the New Jersey State

Employment Service." "Her mother retired as the treasurer of the hospitality committee to the United Nations." "His mother is a real estate agent in San Marino."

As brides, these mothers had been poised between the time when women in their class stayed home and when they went out to work. I say "their class" because the *New York Times* did not, and does not, list all the weddings in its geographical area, by any means. It seems, in the wedding pages, to be something of a record of the East Coast elite, of Ivy Leaguers, of doctors, lawyers, diplomats, and their children. Which is why my father-in-law wanted us in there so badly he pulled a few strings—and also why he had to pull them. The wedding of a farmer and a writer/editor from Albany, Dartmouth graduates or not, was something of a stretch. Let's just say there was no photograph.

So we were the outer edge of the elite, and so were my parents (whose engagement announcement appeared in the *Times*), the daughter of an Atlanta almanac publisher and the son of an ob/gyn from Montgomery. But still we were in the elite, and so were they, and the female place in that world was ambivalent in 1967; was she a socialite and hostess, or was she a high-powered careerist? Of Mrs. Ralph S. Mosely, the former Abigail Sturges, the *Times* wrote in 1967, "She was presented in 1962 at the New York Junior League Debutante Ball and at the Christmas Ball. She is assistant art director of Progressive Architecture magazine." Over and over you read of debuts and presentations into society—of preparations for a decorative life; and then, over and over, of college degrees and future careers.

"Future" is the key, I think; in that respect Mrs. Mosely, firmly established in her career already when she married, was an anomaly in those pages. Mostly these couples were marrying at the beginning of their professional lives; the median age at which a man first married in 1967 was 23.1

years; for a woman it was 20.6. In 1997 it was 26.8 for men and 25 for women. More often than not, those brides and grooms from 1967 were still getting their college or graduate degrees, or were about to join such-and-such a firm or about to take up such-and-such an appointment. "He and his wife will serve with the Peace Corps in Cameroon, Africa." In the *Times* wedding pages that came out on our wedding day, everyone seems to be in their late twenties and early thirties, with a couple of fifty-year-olds sprinkled in (ages were given in these pages; they weren't in 1967). They've already done the Peace Corps, and they've been living together in Manhattan—or so the reader infers, since their plans for the future are rarely mentioned. They're in their future already. Not so in the sixties: "After a wedding trip to Jamaica, the couple will live in New York"; "The couple will live in Port Washington"; "He and his bride, after a honeymoon in Acapulco, Mexico, will make their home in Austin."

My new life began years before my wedding, when I moved in with Adam in college; no rattling cans tied to my fender alerted the world to the momentous occasion. Later, when I graduated and moved to Albany to be with Adam, I didn't get new underwear or new pots and pans or a party. No formal announcements went out, no listing in the local paper. Wouldn't that be wonderful, if they reported the really important stuff? "Carrie Holsinger, daughter of Jan and Robert Holsinger of Timberville, Va., announced in a brief family discussion last week that she would no longer study dentistry. She will instead devote herself to her interest in fly-fishing. Carrie wore a white cotton tank top and green shorts to the discussion, and was accompanied by her best friend, Susan, and her older sister, Renee." "Peter Gould, son of Jackie Gould and the late Arnold Gould III of Seattle, Wash., woke with a start this morning and admitted to himself the true nature of his sexual orientation. Peter, 22, a graduate of Wesleyan University, called his sister, Liz, soon thereafter."

My mother says that it finally hit her that Adam and I were living together when she saw my toothbrush on his bathroom sink. Which is the opposite of a public announcement and a celebration: a small detail observed in the most private room in the house. I took this enormous step in my life on tiptoe, while no one was looking. When I moved my belongings into Adam's place, I explained it as practical: we could concentrate on our work better if we weren't always thinking about when we'd see each other next; plus, we saved on rent. That was that. No commitment to a passionate love, no risky public acknowledgment of the change I was making in my life, no romance. I know that I am lucky to have a mother who cared enough about me to visit me regularly at college, and yet whose only concern about my moving in with Adam was that a breakup would leave me with an awkward home life. Lucky to have parents so close and yet so noncontrolling. But their liberal-mindedness made the transition away from single life even less perceptible: I didn't even have a family fight to mark the occasion.

And then I moved to Albany after college because I wanted to be with Adam, and he couldn't very well move the farm. Albany was as good a place as any to get a job; I had no other plans or places to go. But, of course, I had no other plans because I chose not to make any. My father took exception to this: his hyperachieving academic daughter forgot to apply for a Rhodes scholarship; his thoroughbred was putting herself out to pasture on a hay farm. So I got my family fight, which consisted mostly of my father's venting his worry and frustration, and my taking insult and pretending I knew exactly what I was doing with my life.

But somewhere along the way—without a ring, without a

proposal, without a press release—I had decided to spend the rest of my life with Adam. Maybe it was the third time I met him, in passing on a cold day in Hanover, and he kissed me lightly on the cheek with warm, soft lips. Or maybe it was when I met his older brother, an avid reader, a foreign-film lover, a foodie—everything I'd imagined I'd marry—and thought to myself that I'd rather have him as a friend and Adam as a lover. Or maybe it was the first time I felt real pride when I watched him talk to someone, pride in his honesty, directness, intelligence, engagement. Or maybe it was the one time I felt the touch of someone else's skin and knew I had to choose. Maybe I decided to spend the rest of my life with him then.

Or maybe I simply never decided *not* to. Certainly there was no deliberative period following a proposal, no suspense-breaking "Yes!" After seven years of sliding into forever, seven years of nesting, of greater and greater physical and mental familiarity, it seemed as if we'd long ago agreed to marry. The decision wasn't so much, Will I or won't I? as Memorial Day or Labor Day?

What is announced in the paper—the wedding—and what constitutes the real transitional moment in our lives are not necessarily the same anymore. That disjunction is caused, as much as anything, by what sociologists call "cohabitation," as in, "More than half of all first marriages are now preceded by cohabitation." That's according to a 1999 article in the *Economist*. More and more, couples are living together outside of marriage; the number is almost eight times as great as when my parents married. This tendency to live together seems to be the big shift in marriage trends in the twentieth century, rather than the tendency to marry later in life. Couples wedding a hundred years ago were actually at about the same age when they married as we are now (our sense that people married much younger comes from more recent history: the median marriage age dropped precipitously around World War II and has since been climbing back up). So it's not marriage age that's really changed; it's the number of people who live together before they marry. Most people marrying in 1890 would not have already established a household together. Yes, there were couples who lived together outside the laws of state and church; more often than not, though, those couples never married officially—they had common-law marriages. During the world wars, the number of cohabiting couples dropped because common-law wives of soldiers found that they did not receive the same benefits as wives who could produce marriage certificates. The cohabitation rate dropped further after World War II, when renewed prosperity in America allowed more people to marry younger; there was also at that time a concerted effort to glorify marriage and domesticity in order to get women to leave the labor force. In England in the 1950s only one percent of women marrying for the first time lived with their grooms for an extended period first. Figures were similar in the United States, where state statutes against fornication, or sex between unmarried people, were quite common until the 1970s, though few people actually got arrested for it. (About a third of all states still have these laws on the books; no one, apparently, wants to be the state legislator to champion the legalization of extramarital sex.) In the late 1960s, when my parents married, just eight percent of marriages were preceded by cohabitation. But times have changed and continue to change: now the figure is more than half, and growing. In America, living together before marriage has become the norm rather than the exception.

Demographics have a lot to do with it. We hit puberty earlier than ever, become sexually active earlier than ever, and spend longer getting educated and settling into careers before we marry. Which leaves us as single, sexually active adults for an extended period, in a culture in which premarital sex has become widely accepted. Despite the demographics, though, some social commentators, like the conservative radio psychologist Laura Schlessinger, argue that cohabitation is a sign of rashness and self-indulgence. "Having sex too soon, moving in without commitments or similar goals, are the behaviors of basically immature, let-me-feel-good-right-now people." We cohabitors are like greedy children, who want our candy before we eat our peas, or instead of our peas. This doesn't make sense to me, though, because if we're so immature, so hedonistic, why don't we just live at our respective homes, have our parents pay our rents and buy our snacks, and then meet our lovers for sex? Since premarital sex is hardly taboo in most American circles now—since you *can* eat your candy before your vegetables—why toss in the hassles of making a home together, of chores and responsibilities, of bills to pay? And if you're too old to live with your parents, still it must be easier to live alone or with a roommate you can ignore than with a lover whose moods and desires require your attention.

Most of the people I know who are living together, or who did, before they married (I can think of very few couples who haven't) *are* committed to one another; their delay in marrying reflects more caution than impatience. They are making sure they are suited to one another, live well together, are ready to wed. Cohabitation today in America is something like the old European betrothal, a period, between the ring exchange and before the wedding ceremony, during which the couple learned to know each other, their future marriage decided but not yet legally binding. It was, as cohabitation often is now, an extended transition between the single and the married state, between the world of childhood and the world of adulthood. Some people who live together do so instead of marrying, yes; but an estimated sixty percent of cohabiting couples end up getting married. They are just practicing first.

Now that it is socially acceptable to practice marriage, it seems almost rash and immature *not* to. Now it's the people who marry without having lived together who seem to be the impatient ones. When my older sister, Amy, called me back in 1993 to tell me she was getting married, I congratulated her, but I worried over it: she had lived with her fiancé only briefly, in college. Why not take a year or two to see if you live well together? I wanted to ask. Chris's parents might not have liked them to; his father, a Lutheran minister, probably believed a wedding should precede cohabitation. But they wouldn't have stood in their son's way. Amy and Chris could have lived together without repercussion, they could have practiced.

But, to be honest, though Adam and I would end up marrying, I can't say that when we moved in together we considered it to be simply a trial period before marriage. After a year or so together, it was pretty clear we were headed in that direction. But when we moved in with each other about three months after we started dating, marriage was definitely not on our minds. Living together just made sense: with two homebodies who want to spend all their time together, there's only one option. Or two, I should say: move in together or get married and move in together. Get married after three months? If we'd even considered it, we would have thought it was nuts. Move in? Well, you can always move out. It just seemed like the natural thing to do.

When I moved to Albany to be with Adam, the nature of our living together changed a bit. In college, we had had other roommates as well, we were moving as often as every semester, we were somewhere else in the summer. Every three months there was a clear moment of transition, a moment when we could say, This isn't working—I'm going to look for a new place. After college, our life together took on a new stability. For the four and a half years before we married we lived in the same house together, making brunch on the weekend, taking out the trash on Monday, getting Chinese take-out once a week. We had certain sides of the bed, a certain spot next to the telephone for unpaid bills, a certain routine we followed when we left the house on trips. We were set in our ways, almost a caricature of a married couple.

So why weren't we married? If, after a few years, Adam and I had gotten in a good deal of practice, if we had been assuming for years that we would be together for the rest of our lives, why hadn't we made it official? After we began acting for a while more married than most married people, our parents began to agitate about a wedding date. Adam's father's agitation took the form of open nagging; my father avoided the topic with exaggerated courtesy. But everyone was waiting. Our families could tell we'd chosen each other—it was obvious. So what were we waiting for?

This was not merely a hypothetical question we mused over in the bathtub; this was a question to which we had to respond. At my sister's wedding, we counted thirty-two hints, nudges, insinuations, and direct questions, as in, "So, when are you two tying the knot?" and "Does this give you any ideas?" and "Taking notes?" and "I'm looking forward to the next one, if you know what I mean." Yes, we knew what you meant.

We didn't really know what we were waiting for, or how to articulate it. But we did feel that the longer we waited, the more meaningful our wedding would have to be. If a wedding automatically follows courtship and precedes cohabitation, if a wedding constitutes real change in someone's life—as it did when my parents married—then the details don't matter quite so much, the significance lies in the fact of the wedding, rather than in the way that fact is articulated. But if the wedding is more a statement than a deed, if it comes in the middle of two people's lives together, then every choice, every decision would mean something about those two people. That's an intimidating thought.

I joked once that our guests would have waited so long for our wedding that when it finally happened, they were bound to expect that we'd been spending our prewedding years writing our vows in sonnet form. I complained that the only reception that could satisfy so many years of antici- pation would be catered sumptuously by the bride in a synagogue built by the groom, the two of whom would metamorphose into a Jewish Astaire and Rogers for their first dance.

It was a joke, but it wasn't far from how I felt, from how much bigger the Big Event seemed to get as the years passed. That's why we put off wedding, I guess. But we could have avoided those issues with a quick trip to the justice of the peace. The real question is why we put off *being married*. The answer is related, I think: we wanted to be ready, to make sure we were going to do it right.

Eventually, in order to wed, I had to give up my secret plan to learn Hebrew so that I could write my wedding vows in a sacred language. But I was tempted—I wanted to be that prepared. Likewise we wanted our relationship to be just right before we publicly named it "marriage." Adam and I thought our commitment to each other was so important, we wanted to make sure it would hold together. If it could hold without the extra support of official recognition and the prospect of a messy divorce, surely it would hold *with* those things as well. It was almost as if we wanted to have the best marriage possible before saying, "Hey, everyone, we're married!"

And we're not alone in this desire, not today, and not historically. In Britain in the early 1800s, common-law spouses were called "tally" couples. The historian John Gillis writes,

> [The] term *tally* . . . suggested a partnership based on some degree of affection. When any couple quarreled it was said, "they don't tally well together," implying that . . . tally couples were regarded as particularly well matched, there being nothing but their mutual agreement to keep them together.

After having nothing but our mutual agreement keep us together for more than seven years before we married, we felt pretty sure we had a solid thing. We'd been to weddings where we weren't in the least bit sure that the couples marrying would stay that way; we wanted our union to feel certain to our guests. "I'm not worried about you two at all," said a friend, after rehearsing his doubts about the two weddings he would attend before ours. "You guys are a sure bet."

I think people who live together before they marry are often giving *more* weight and significance to wedding and marriage, not less. They wait and they practice, until they feel their marriage will be a sure bet.

There is a trade-off, though. In eliminating risk, in eliminating the unknown, Adam and I had eliminated romance. We had no doubt, and therefore we had no cold feet, no jitters, no nausea, and no locking ourselves in separate bathrooms during the honeymoon and moaning, "What was I *doing* when I said 'I do'?" But we had no honeymoon either. Literally or figuratively. And when I think about my parents flying from Atlanta to New York directly after their reception, spending the night at the Regency and the next two months or so in Europe learning to be with one another, breakfast to lunch to dinner to breakfast, I'm a little envious.

No practice and no safety net. It must have been exhilarating.

Today, fewer and fewer couples who marry have that exhilarating sense of risk. In America. But since a combination of religious and economic factors keeps Italian twenty-somethings at home far longer than their American counterparts, we do have Italian friends who didn't have the option of living together. We met Paolo and Silvia during the spring in Florence, and they came to visit us that summer before we married. They told us they were planning to marry too, the following year, and so we talked about wedding parties and parental involvement and Italian versus American wedding etiquette. As the four of us chatted, Adam and I moved about preparing dinner; we had hosted so many guests in our home, given so many parties together, we had long ago divided up the chores, long ago dispensed with the need to discuss who should do what, or indeed what should be done. Adam picked and shucked the corn, grilled the chicken I had readied, and set the picnic table under the maple in the front yard; I turned the marinade into a sauce, steamed the corn, and made a salad while my biscuits baked. All four of us were happy and excited about our upcoming weddings; but only Paolo and Silvia were excited about their upcoming marriage. They had been dating, in love, for four years, but sleeping in single beds in their parents' homes on different sides of the Arno. They couldn't wait to sleep together every night in a double bed in *their* apartment. They couldn't wait to set up home together, to cook and clean and welcome guests together. To be married. They couldn't wait to have what we had already.

When my sister, Amy, and Chris decided to marry, with no practice and no safety net, they weren't forced to do so by social or religious constraint as were our parents and our Florentine friends. They could have lived together first. But at that moment, living on opposite coasts, after having broken up once and then recommitting, my sister and the man she loved wanted a fresh start, a sense of beginning a new life together, a "from now on." And having their toothbrushes hang side by side just wasn't enough.

Adam and I wouldn't get a new start or a new home; when our thirtieth wedding anniversary rolls around, it will seem as if someone had miscounted. Part of me wished that our first year of marriage would be more like Paolo and Silvia's, alive with the joy of living together at last. Part of me yearned for the exhilaration that our kind of wedding, the modern American cohabitors' wedding, simply could not provide.

And we weren't losing just the exhilaration, I thought; we were losing some of the significance. I felt almost foolish calling people to tell them I was getting married, as if they had been in suspense about whether or not Adam and I would decide to commit. When the gifts started coming in that June, I was surprised not only because they implied that our home together would be a new home, but also because they implied that our wedding was a momentous occasion. Wedding just wasn't going to produce as serious a change in our lives as it would for Paolo and Silvia, as it had for my parents or my sister. And because of that, I thought, it could not have the same gravity.

As compensation for this loss, could I say our marriage would be more secure, statistically speaking? Do cohabitors have a better chance at a stable, happy marriage, once they finally wed? Apparently not: David Myers writes in *The Pursuit of Happiness*, "Successful trial marriages do *not* predict a successful marriage," and the research backs him up. A 1990 Gallup survey on love and marriage revealed that "those who have cohabited are less likely . . . to say that their marriage is very happy and that their spouse is their best friend, though they are as likely as those who did not cohabit to say they would enter the same marriage again." What would explain this statistic? One sociologist, the priest and columnist Andrew Greeley, concludes that we cohabitors have, "it would seem, less respect for and commitment to marriage and to the bond of sexual union." Perhaps. Perhaps we are also more likely to think about and be critical of our own relationships; we don't believe that marrying is the beginning of a new and perfect life, that our spouse is always the center of that life, that we are bound to be happy ever after. I think the fascinating point is that we *are* as likely as those who hadn't practiced first to say we would marry the same person again, though we are more circumspect about the state of our marriages. No, I'm not deliriously happy, those who had cohabited were saying, but no, I'm not likely to be deliriously happy with someone else, either.

People who live together before they marry do end up divorcing more than those who don't, however. Citing divorce rates of former cohabitors, another survey suggests that "an extended period of cohabitation can be in some way detrimental to a resulting marriage." Studies have shown that we cohabitors have anything from a 33 to a 100 percent higher rate of separation or divorce than those who don't cohabit. And researchers try to explain this phenomenon by arguing that cohabitors don't take marriage as seriously as non-cohabitors, even after they marry. Few consider the possibility that if a couple has the freedom to live together before marriage, they are unlikely, as a group, to be constrained by religious and cultural taboos against divorce. In other words, how many fundamentalist Muslims, strict Catholics, or Orthodox Jews divorce? And how many of those cohabited first?

This is what sociologists call the "selection effect." The selection effect causes many statistics that might otherwise be worrying. Did you know that couples in which men are more likely to share household tasks with their wives are significantly more likely to get divorced? Think about that one for a minute. Should men, for the sake of their marriages, retreat to the sofa and call for their slippers? Of course not. Are the men who do, and the women who come running, likely to be from a social sector less tolerant of divorce? I think so. The selection effect may explain the more shocking rates of increase in marital instability for cohabitors. But a few studies have tried to control for the selection effect, and they still found that cohabitation has a negative impact on future marriage—or at the very least, that it makes "no positive contribution" to it. Maybe practice doesn't make perfect, after all.

The point is that no matter how sure you try to be, even if you wait until the middle of your life, until your home and the love it holds are long established, there is no such thing as a sure bet. When you wed, you are still making a change, however subtle, between "This is who we are" to "This is who we will be." And there is always risk in that. Maybe the stakes are even higher: If you have seven years of practice, by the time you say, "We're ready," people believe it, expect it to be true. If you choose to marry *because* you have made a life together and not *in order to*, you are making a claim for your own stability as a couple. Even though your chances of lasting are really no better, and may even be worse, than anyone else's.

We had plenty of practice, and *then* we took away the safety net. The most we knew for sure before we took it away was that for more than seven years, Adam and I tallied well together, more than four of those here in this house where we would live when we got married.

Only it wouldn't be exactly the same house. Its insides were gradually changing, shifting to accommodate the influx of gifts not to Adam or me, but to us, the soon-to-be newly wed. I never felt I deserved these presents, however grateful I was for them. But I began as they accumulated to be grateful *to* them, for bringing some sense of a new marriage, with its risks and its rewards, into our old home.

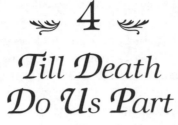

4

Till Death
Do Us Part

The rate of divorce is not in itself an argument against marriage, any more than the number of bad poems is an argument against poetry. The risk of failure is not to be avoided.

—FERDINAND MOUNT

I had been up addressing invitations for two hours in nothing but a big T-shirt; it was around nine. I straightened up, stretched my neck, and decided to get dressed. But when I walked into our bedroom, it was dark and cool, and Adam was still in semisleep on his belly, arms around his pillow, left knee bent, sheet tangled around his hips. I couldn't resist. When I climbed in, he turned onto his side, away from me, and I turned onto my side too and then wriggled myself into place, the tops of my thighs touching the backs of his, his bottom in my groin. I pulled my T-shirt up so I could feel the skin of my stomach against the skin of his back. I placed my nose between his shoulder blades and breathed.

I thought, Please let me die before he does.

It was the middle of the summer, two months before the wedding, and I had started to think about death. That may sound odd, but a wedding is the first time in life that one publicly and officially acknowledges death as a possibility. The words float past as familiar as Mendelssohn's wedding march: "till death do us part." One book on writing your own vows suggests not mentioning death during the ceremony: "For most people, the word 'death' has negative connotations," explains the author, Peg Kehret. "It is not a happy word." The book suggests promising to stay together "for all the days of my life" instead, or "as long as I live." But even those words contain the idea that life is finite. It is of course possible to write vows that avoid naming either death or the idea that life has a time limit, but even if you manage not to speak of it, death hovers at the wedding: think of all the legal aspects of marriage that are connected to death. According to the U.S. General Accounting Office, there are over one thousand legal benefits, rights, and privileges contingent on marital status, and many of them concern death. Your spouse is the person who will survive and bury you and inherit your property, or whom you will survive and bury and whose property you will inherit. The married widow or widower picks the epitaph, receives Social Security benefits, and pays no inheritance taxes on the house, the car, and the bank account. He or she can sue for wrongful death, collect unpaid wages, choose whether to donate the organs of the deceased. The list goes on and on. Friends of ours who used to see no point in getting married (and several philosophical points in *not* getting married) ended up, after buying their first house and before having their first child, in a judge's chambers signing the papers. Why? They didn't suddenly believe in the institution of marriage; they wanted the right to sit at the death bed in the hospital room, the right to the kids after the funeral, the right to inherit. Death, in a suit and tie and carrying a briefcase full of papers, stood with them as they stood before the judge.

Death's presence at a wedding isn't just an official one; it's a personal one too. You or your spouse will be the center of the other's mourning, and the central caretaker of the other's memory. When you marry, you choose your representative on earth after you have died or your representative in the afterworld (if you believe in one) after he or she has. Maybe this sounds morbid; it certainly sounds melancholy. But I think the presence of death is part of what gives a wedding its solemnity, its weight. And sad as it may be, there is joy in choosing the person whose death I will administer, or who will administer mine. It is the ultimate honor that I can bestow on someone, and I took pleasure in the prospect of bestowing it on the person who, in my adult life, had loved me best while knowing me best. Who knew me completely—knew the me that knocked into furniture, withered before male authority, lied to avoid blame, worried about being fat, declined to play for fear she would lose—and, miraculously, still loved me. That person should be the one to comfort me as I die and remember me in my death, and that person, though I refused to consider it beyond the mindless ease of a parallel clause, was the person I wanted to comfort as he died and remember in his death. And that's one of the reasons that I planned to marry him.

When I married him, I would renounce, implicitly or explicitly, all former notions of my own immortality. Even if part of me still believed that I was immortal (and how many of us fully, actively, consistently comprehend that one day we will die?), marrying was going to challenge that belief.

And that's true now, early in the twenty-first century. Imagine how present death must have been at weddings a hundred, two hundred, five hundred years ago. When women routinely died in childbirth, when pneumonia could kill you if you hadn't died already from the flu. When you married, you might reasonably expect your marriage to last ten or twenty years, and you would certainly expect death to be what ended it. "Till death do us part" was a statement not of determined togetherness but of inescapable fact.

Perhaps at the end of the twentieth century, death isn't exactly stepping on the train of the gown or catching on the tail of the morning coat as bride and groom walk down the aisle, but he's there, along with his guest, limitation. If your wedding reminds you that your life has a time limit, it teaches you for perhaps the first time that your life has other limits as well. For one thing, immortality and infinite possibility go hand in hand: if you live forever, there is a chance that you can experience and accomplish all that you wish. You may yet learn Chinese, manage a baseball team, live on the Left Bank. But when you accept that you are mortal, you have to accept that more than just your time on earth is limited. Or rather, you have to accept that limited time limits your life. You have to choose between learning Chinese and learning to play the hammer dulcimer. You simply do not have time to do it all.

So marrying brings a consciousness of death, and death, as a practical matter, forces you to choose to be and do some things rather than others. But marrying carries with it even more limitation, unrelated to the ticking of the clock. When you marry, when you accept someone else as a partner in your life, you limit your choice of spouse, of course. You also commit yourself to a certain life, or if not to a certain life then at least to a certain person, whose desires and decisions are bound to conflict with, and thus limit, your own. That trip to China may not intrigue your spouse; two months apart may interest him or her even less. Every decision you make is now a compromise; your notion that life is rife with possibility is therefore compromised as well. Hence we get the stereotypical image of the midlife crisis: a married man, finding he has more gray than brown hairs on his head, realizes suddenly that he is heading toward death and tries to ward it off with a new hobby, or lover, or all-terrain vehicle. He is trying to assert that all the possibilities are still open to him, that his choices are unlimited, despite the fact that he has settled into one job and lives in one house in one town with one woman, two kids, and a goldfish.

When you marry, you officially give up both immortality and infinite possibility. There is, of course, an escape clause: divorce. With divorce, we mean to be able to reclaim infinite possibility. The wide world of women or men is open again, all points of the globe call out for us to reside there; once more we can be whoever we want. The notion of immortality is harder to reclaim, but we do speak of our divorced selves as "starting a new life," which comforts us with the thought that if the life we know ends, we can simply begin again.

The phrase *till death do us part* may have been haunting me before we wed because it reminded me of my own mortality, but it haunted Adam because it conjured up the specter of divorce. If death didn't part us, divorce would. In the days in late June when we addressed our wedding invitations, two impending divorces were on our minds, both of them closer to Adam than to me. One was not unexpected: the couple—I'll call them the Swifts—had been together six years, but they had long since stopped appearing to enjoy each other's company. We hadn't been particularly optimistic even at their wedding, which seemed to us too hasty and unbalanced: a step he yearned to take and she figured she could always take back, especially since they weren't planning on having children. That summer we learned she *was* taking it back; we addressed the invitation to her new apartment, since it was she who was a childhood friend of Adam's. Omitting her husband's name from the envelope seemed like a momentous thing to do, as if we were implicitly erasing him from our lives, implicitly separating the Swifts even more.

The other marital failure came as a shock. A family Adam had known since he was in first grade was splitting up. This family had seemed as stable—more stable—than any family I knew. The conflicts I witnessed in the Stables' home, where Adam and I had dinner almost every week, were as trivial as a sitcom's: the kids begged to stay up past their bedtime, or fought over toys, or whined about whose video would go in the VCR. Maybe one parent complained once or twice about the other's failure to complete a chore. Maybe. But mostly they seemed to work a magical middle-class blend of the fifties and the nineties: she baked for the PTA; he cleaned out the pool; they took turns driving the kids to soccer practice. When we sat around their kitchen table, we didn't talk about a great deal *other* than soccer practice, and sometimes it got a bit monotonous playing family board games for hours, but at least it was safe and secure. Or so we thought.

We addressed the invitation to the whole family, to the house where we had attended more harmonious poolside barbecues and Christmas parties and Easter brunches than I could count. On that envelope, I guess, we were implicitly willing the Stables to stay together, to be what they once were, what we, what Adam especially, still needed to believe they were. Adam had clung to them most at moments when *his* parents' marriage hit a rocky patch; they had been his lifeboat. So when their marriage was about to capsize, he saw it as proof that anyone's could. Even that ours could. After all, the fact that we had lived together happily for years was no proof that we would continue to.

When I frowned at Adam's pessimism, he cited the statistic that everyone cites: half of all marriages end in divorce. How could we be sure, he asked me, that ours wouldn't? What made us so special? How could we promise to love each other always; who knew what lay ahead? If the Stables could fall apart, despite having three kids, a Catholic background, and a firm belief in family, why couldn't we?

"You're right," I would say, "you're absolutely right," in a flat, low voice that meant, You're right in a technical, unromantic sort of a way, and if that's the sort of person you want to be, *I'm* certainly not going to change your mind. But I was too cowardly to say what I really felt, which was, We *are* going to stick. I just know it. It's not a matter of beating the odds; it's a matter of being on the right side of them, and my confidence and determination are such that even if it were nine to one, I would cheerfully peg myself as a one. But you don't say that sort of thing out loud; it sounds foolish and arrogant.

Which was part of Adam's point. He knew when I said, "you're right," I really meant, "you're wrong." And he thought I was willfully ignoring the evidence. Didn't I realize that almost every couple that ends up divorcing believed at the moment they married that they were going to be together forever? The Swifts were the rare exception (or rather Mrs. Swift, because, even in their case, Mr. Swift had believed it would last). The Stables were the rule, however: on their wedding day, twenty years before their marriage broke apart, they felt exactly the optimism and determination I was feeling now. Shouldn't that tell me something?

In all of what I imagine to be their confusion and guilt and embarrassment, the Stables stopped speaking to us. I felt bad for Adam; these people were his adopted family, part of his childhood as well as his adulthood. But I felt worse for their children, for whom Adam had been first babysitter, first softball coach, first crush, first grown-up friend. A year before, it would have been unthinkable for them to miss our wedding; a year before, we worried about how to tell the littlest Stable that we weren't planning on having a flower girl. In a month we would get a reply card that read simply, "Sorry the Stables are unable to attend."

I hurt for the kids, and I questioned the wisdom of the parents. Both Adam's and my parents have intact first marriages, but both marriages, at one time or another, would have qualified, at least from the outside, for "Wouldn't divorce be better than *this*?" status. And now both seemed to be happy marriages. So if the Stables had just stuck it out . . . wouldn't it have been better?

That even troubled marriage is preferable to divorce is an idea that has gained much currency in the last decade or so. A movement has begun, in fact, to change the divorce laws to make it more difficult to end marriages. The divorce reform movement, which started in the early 1990s, aims to revoke or limit no-fault divorce laws. First enacted in California in 1970, no-fault divorce allows couples to end their marriages without assigning blame for the break-up, without accusing each other of adultery or abuse; they can simply say that the marriage isn't working, and after a specified waiting period, end it. No-fault divorce, which obviated the need in many cases for protracted court battles and private investigators, made divorce easier and cheaper. Every state in the union has such laws. But bills in Michigan, Washington, and Montana, among others, had recently proposed abolishing them. Georgia, Oklahoma, and Idaho state legislatures had considered proposals for longer waiting periods and mandatory marriage counseling; Louisiana and Arkansas had passed laws establishing the option for couples to have a "covenant marriage," which would be harder to break than the regular kind.

The argument behind these proposed changes is that divorce is so easy to get it encourages people to give up on their marriages sooner than they should. Hence the divorce rate is out of control; as everyone says, one out of two marriages will end in divorce. But everyone is wrong. That number is based on 1990 U.S. Census data that said 2.4 million marriages were performed that year and 1.2 million divorces were filed. But given the 54 million marriages already existing and *not* breaking up that year, that really doesn't mean one out of two at all. The actual percentage of U.S. marriages that end in divorce is unclear: I've read, in reputable sources, everything from 12.5 to 43. I'm not a statistician or a sociologist, but the consensus seems to gather around a rate in the low forties, and dropping.

Anyway, it *feels* as if every other marriage breaks up, and that is what a lot of reform advocates seem to be reacting to—a general sense that, in contrast to a simple past in which men and women married for life, we live in a complicated, divorce-torn present, in which children have to spend three and a half days per week at each parent's house, lawyers get rich over bitter settlements, and the bride and groom cross their fingers when they say, "till death do us part." What does seem to be true is that divorce has ill effects on the children involved. Studies implicate divorce in higher high-school dropout rates, higher teen pregnancy rates, in more childhood poverty, depression, and even teen suicide. The numbers are tricky, though, because to whom are children of divorced parents being compared? Usually, it's to children of intact marriages, both the happy ones and the unhappy ones. It would seem fairer to compare them to children only of unhappy marriages; sure it's healthier to live in a happy home than a broken one, but how healthy is it to live in a home full of the tension and hostility of a marriage that isn't working? Isn't that the real choice people are making? And, too, people who divorce tend to start with more problems than people who don't; that is, if a father is an alcoholic, and as an alcoholic, statistically more likely to divorce, couldn't that, rather than the divorce itself, be the source of a child's depression?

Still, if I look only at the Stables, and the fact that not only Adam but most of the adults who'd had a part in the kids' lives for years were pushed away from them, I could tell you that divorce hurts kids. That is why some people advocate divorce reform.

But divorce isn't a new problem, as those reformers would have us believe. Divorce isn't a result of the crazy sixties; people have been splitting up since marriage was invented. Ancient cultures clearly tolerated divorce, though they often made it far easier for the man to obtain than the woman, and for the rich man to obtain than the poor one. But one sociologist, Ferdinand Mount, goes as far as to say, "The most regular and universal feature of non-Christian or pre-Christian marriage is the relative ease of divorce." In Western Europe, after disdaining marriage as a poor second to celibacy, the (Catholic) Church finally declared it a sacrament in 1215, essentially taking control of it, and making divorce much more difficult. Even when marriages were under strong church control, though, people found ways to end them. They just didn't do it officially. In Shropshire and Wales in the 1800s, for instance, the lower classes believed that if a husband failed to support his wife, she could simply give him back the wedding ring, and she would be free to marry again.

So divorce seems to be about as modern as sex. The rate did, however, rise steadily throughout the twentieth century (with the exception of the 1950s), and it does seem that no-fault provisions in the early seventies spurred the increase further. But did making divorce easier really end marriages, or did it just make their endings official? Some argue that the rate of unofficial separation and abandonment in the late nineteenth century is close to today's divorce rate.

Those no-fault divorce laws may simply have allowed more people to turn de facto divorces into de jure ones, to define legally a split that had already taken place. And they may have come along at just the right moment. A lot of changes occurred in America in the late sixties and early seventies, most notably the fact that women joined the work force in unprecedented numbers. Certainly the increase in freedom and earning power for women permitted more of them to decide to go it alone if they felt they needed to. Judith Stacey writes that working outside the home "reduced some of women's economic dependency on men, and thus, has weakened one coercive buttress of marriage." Coercion and inequality, she argues, supported marriage in the past; now, "women's capacity to survive outside marriage, however meagerly, explains why [the divorce rate] rose so sharply in recent decades. Marriage became increasingly fragile as it became less economically obligatory, particularly for women." Certainly our friend Mrs. Swift would have thought twice before marrying, and three times before divorcing, if she had been supported financially by her husband. And in fact she waited to divorce until she had completed a graduate degree, until her earning potential was higher, which points to the part that money plays in these decisions. Women in general are also more likely than men to initiate divorce, which gives their increased freedom an even stronger correlation to an increased divorce rate.

Historically, when divorces are more difficult to obtain, it's those with power and money who manage to sway the system in their favor; you had to be wealthy or well-connected to get a papal dispensation. No-fault divorce laws didn't create divorce; they merely extended the right to all. Which means, more divorces. Mount argues that the divorce rate has increased over the last few decades because the working classes can now afford it as easily as the upper classes. He adds, "Free and universal access to divorce is something quite new in the Christian era—as remarkable a social change as free and universal access to reliable contraception."

This analogy would not reassure social conservatives. And yet it is apt, since the wide availability of contraception is blamed for the prevalence of teen sex, just as the wide availability of divorce is blamed for the breakdown of the family. No-fault divorce, reformers argue, has devalued marriage, making it a casual, commitment-free affair, "a lifestyle choice." "With no-fault divorce," said an Ohio legislator in favor of changing the law, "marriage has become little more than notarized dating." John Crouch, a divorce lawyer and advocate of reform, griped, "Getting married in America is like doing business in Russia. Everything is up for grabs, everything is constantly renegotiated, and nobody has to keep their word."

Wait a minute. "Nobody has to keep their word." That's freedom, right? Isn't that a good thing? Maybe if we could really make people honor their vows, if we could really make people love one another, support one another, till death, it would be worth giving up freedom. But the truth is, we can't force people to honor their vows the way we can force people to honor business contracts. All we can do, by toughening the divorce laws, is force people to *pretend* to honor their vows, force them to stay together, or stay together longer, when the marriage is already broken.

With no-fault divorce, nobody *has* to stay in a marriage he or she doesn't want to be in; nobody *has* to live with a mistake. Is such a concept simply a product of the era of personal gratification, self-actualization, and irresponsibility in which we live? This is what John Milton wrote on the topic, around 1645: "It is no less than cruelty to force a man to remain in that state as the solace of his life, which he and his friends know will be either the undoing or the disheartening of his life. " Milton believed that marriage was too important, too central to a man's life, *not* to allow divorce. He's not talking about cases of abuse, abandonment, adultery; he's talking about 1990s suburban-variety incompatibility.

> That indisposition, unfitness, or contrariety of mind, arising from a cause in nature unchangeable, hindering, and ever likely to hinder the main benefits of conjugal society, which are solace and peace, is a greater reason of divorce than natural frigidity, especially if there be no children, and that there be mutual consent.

Milton hesitates on the question of children. So do I. That is why the Swifts' divorce, as unhappy as it was, was so much less troubling than the Stables' divorce. I don't know why the Stables broke up; I hope before they did they thought long and hard about the effect it would have on their children. Maybe they made a terrible mistake; maybe, even if they made the right choice for themselves, they made the wrong choice for their kids. Theirs wasn't a hostile, tense marriage, the kind of marriage you wouldn't want children growing up around. Theirs was the kind of marriage reformers point to when they say it should be harder to divorce: the kind that seems to be working well enough. But I can't judge who should have to stay together whether they want to or not, and lawmakers can't either. I think all parents should read to their kids, and all families should eat their meals at table together; I'll bet if you compared kids from those families to ones who ate alone on the sofa in front of the TV you would find some solid data in support of strict family togetherness and literacy legislation. But you can't make people good parents that way, and you can't make families whole by fiat. I think we have to let the couple decide whether, if their love for one another is gone, they can recover it; whether, if they can't recover it, they should just do without.

Doing without, even for the sake of the kids, isn't what marriage is about, says Milton. "Marriage is a cov'nant the very being whereof consists, not in a forc't cohabitation, and counterfeit performance of duties, but unfained love and peace." If Milton had his way, only the lovelit marriages, only true marriages, would stay together. God, he says, doesn't like the other kind. "Love in marriage cannot live nor subsist unless it be mutual; and where love cannot be, there can be left of wedlock nothing but the empty husk of an outside matrimony, as undelightful and unpleasing to God as any other kind of hypocrisy." Milton was arguing with the Catholic Church and the Church of England. Today, to counter the divorce reform movement, sociologist Ollie Pocs ventured similarly that "the divorce rate has risen *not* because people care less about marriage but because they care *more*. That is, they won't stay in a poor relationship."

"Nobody has to keep their word." We take our commitment to one another into our own hands—out of the church's, out of the law's. We accept the risk. We accept even the risk to our children, whom it is our duty to protect. Mount argues that this acceptance of personal responsibility is part of a general trend, not toward the devaluing of marriage, but toward its exaltation.

> Married couples have taken control of marriage; their weddings are not arranged for them by their families, their parents' permission is not often sought, sometimes the parents are not informed . . . often no religious commitment is sought or given. These outward and visible signs mirror an inner conviction that marriage is too important to allow any outside force to meddle with it;

this Milton-like view raises both the commitment to and the expectation of marriage. When a marriage breaks down, it is as great a fall as Lucifer's.

I guess, when Adam and I discussed divorce, I had hubris as great as Lucifer's. I was proud to think that the only thing holding our marriage together would be us. Our marriage will last, I thought. But not because we could not legally end it, not because I depended on Adam financially and could not leave him, not because we would be excommunicated or shunned if the marriage failed. Our sense of honor, our patience, our maturity, our love would make us keep our word. Faith in marriage—faithfulness within marriage—like faith in God, is meaningless without free will. With free will, it means everything.

Adam was not willing to swear that we would not fail. He is cautious, altogether without hubris. But though we wouldn't swear that death and not divorce would part us, we would allude in our vows to our own mortality, we would tell each other that we were each other's choice for the rest of our lives. That our time was limited, and that we were devoting it to one another. And through that vow, I would glimpse the limits of my life.

We spent the week after we married with some friends at a lake house my grandfather built on Lake Martin outside Montgomery, and there, for the first time, it really hit me. The Lake, as we call it in my family, is a sensual place: the Alabama heat, the slap of wet feet on wood, the light, wrung-out feeling you get after a day of swimming, sunning, and waterskiing, the fact that you spend the days half-naked, half-asleep, half-tipsy. At one point a friend of ours took a nap on the sofa, lying on his back. His body was totally relaxed and open and his breathing was soft and his skin looked cool and smooth, and I wanted to climb onto the sofa with him and put my head on his T-shirted chest. I didn't want to have sex with him—I think the T-shirt was a necessary element of my desire—I just wanted to hold him, love him with the warmth of my body, feel his arm rest lightly on my shoulder. And it seemed unfair to me that I couldn't. I looked accusingly at my wedding ring for a second, but then realized that the ring wasn't what was keeping me off that sofa. It was a commitment to Adam that I'd had for years, it was my friend's girlfriend, it was a social code that doesn't allow my love for a male friend to manifest itself physically.

But it's too easy to blame "society," to shake my fist at the puritanism that pervades America. I would balk too if someone slid into bed next to Adam, with or without sexual intent. Why would that bother me? Maybe because one thing we get when we give up infinite possibility is possession. In return for limiting our choice to one person, we get total security, total confidence that the warmth of our lover's body seeps into our skin, or no one's. The promise, in other words, that he or she has given up infinite possibility too. Along with "till death do us part," we have "I am my beloved's and my beloved is mine," we have "forsaking all others." How many of us are stupid or selfless or saintly enough to accept the limits imposed by marriage for someone who's not willing to do the same for us?

Some people think possession is ugly: my father used to go to elaborate lengths not to say "my wife"; he would introduce my mom as "the woman to whom I am married." Maybe possession is ugly; certainly it has its ugly side. But I think it's a basic human need. I, at least, need it more than I need to believe in infinity. I may have had to limit the possibilities in my life by choosing one person over another, or one person over many; I may have given up the possibility of crossing those few feet to the other couch and claiming someone else's warmth, but I gain thereby the promise that Adam's warmth will always be there for me.

I didn't think that through before I married, but I must have felt it. Because although I was occasionally tempted by someone else's body, or even by someone else's intellectual passion, I was not so foolish as to believe that those things— especially the *promise* of those things—could replace being known and loved as well as Adam knew and loved me, could replace possessing and being possessed by Adam. And how many years and men would it take to find out if someone else could do it? What were the chances that someone else could, what were the chances that I would be so lucky more than once?

I thought about other men ruefully, but not with any real regret. And yet that breathless sense, before one graduates from high school or college, that all the world lies ahead— whatever the actual boundaries of that world might be for each one who feels it—how could I give that up? That I might live anywhere, do anything, be anyone. I had pictured myself in cooking school and writing school, living in London and living at the Lake; all of these possibilities had pulled apart easily with a few tugs of someone else's needs, someone else's life. Could I really give up, officially, my claim on endless possibility?

Yes. I could give it up, I could marry, because I realized that with or without marrying my life had boundaries. I would, finally, live somewhere and be someone. The sense of infinite possibility is a sense of anticipation, of expectation: What will I choose, I, who can choose anything? But choosing itself limits the possibility. So the feeling of infinite possibility carries with it its own destruction; it is inspired by the knowledge that a decision, a narrowing of possibility, must be made. The pleasure of looking at a wide horizon is contained not in the thought that you can stand there looking at a wide horizon forever, but in the thought that you can choose from among all those points to walk toward.

I chose to walk toward a person. Other people walk toward a career, some to an idea of themselves, fewer to an actual place. I didn't know which was right. I considered, once in a while, walking away. But I decided that any way I walked I would feel some sense of loss, that the only way to maintain the sense that I could go anywhere was to go nowhere. So I graduated from college and I walked toward Adam. When we married in August, we would be promising to walk together.

But if we chose some day to walk our separate ways, if we chose to divorce, we could. It wouldn't be that difficult, or expensive, or shameful. If it were, if divorcing would mean we would suffer torment at the hands of our community, or if divorce were simply unobtainable, what would staying together mean about our marriage? Not much. But because we would be free at any moment to walk away, every moment that we walked together would mean we chose to, would mean together is where we wanted to be. Who we wanted to be. And if, with such freedom, we don't part ourselves, if death is indeed what parts us, we will have made a true marriage.

5

Ritual Bath

I had spent twenty minutes on the chrome and purple Nautilus machines discovering that kneading bread had not, in fact, improved my upper body strength. So, trying not to stare at the highly toned women in sports bras and bicycle shorts and perfectly blow-dried hair, I headed back to the stair-steppers. I figured there, at least, I could get pretty far on strength of will. Perched atop a Stairmaster 4000, I adjusted the bandanna I wore to keep the sweat out of my eyes and considered that I probably looked like an out-of-shape pirate. With hips. I closed my eyes and chanted to myself as I started to climb: I'm health-y and attrac-tive, health-y and attrac-tive.

After a while I opened my eyes and glanced at the electronic display between the handgrips to see just how long I had been suffering. One minute and thirty-eight seconds. Across the room a woman stood in front of the mirrors watching herself do curls. She was glorious. Every muscle taut and glistening, her strong upper body tapered to a tiny waist, the kind that lies in contented partnership with span-dex shorts—not a millimeter of extra flesh. Gravity-defying butt, beautifully curved hamstrings and calves, the works. Next to her in the mirror, I could see in the distance a pale, slightly flabby figure in shorts and a baggy T-shirt lurching away on a stepper. It was wearing a blue bandanna.

I shut my eyes. I'm health-y and attrac-tive, health-y and attrac-tive. Two minutes and forty-three seconds.

How did I end up, at the age of twenty-seven, as a provisional member of Gold's Gym, among the thick of neck and thin of thigh? It was early July; in less than two months I was going to walk down the aisle. After consulting with the friend who was turning my Florentine silk into a dress, I understood that I would be walking sleeveless; this was an athletic feat for which I felt I required biceps. But I wasn't toning only my arms at the gym; I was doing the whole circuit. Well, I had just returned from several months in a country where a plateful of pasta constitutes the *first* course. I was out of shape. That was fine for my normal self, but now it wouldn't do at all. Since I was going to be a bride, I wanted to be a perfect bride, and the perfect bride had to have a perfect body.

I was also acutely aware that, of the moments in life in which you are smack at the center of attention—birth, wedding, and death—you are conscious and in control of only one. And so, as you prepare for that moment, the urge can overcome you to unleash your self-improving energies, to present the absolute best you possible, to drop the studied nonchalance with which you may have approached your physical appearance over the years. To get a tan, go on a diet, join a gym. I had assumed all my life that if I were willing to put my mind to it, willing to spend the hours per day necessary, I could have the body I wanted. Same height, of course, and same bones, but somehow the right shape, the shape that men desire and women envy, would form itself around me.

So I'd get in my car on a sunny summer afternoon, drive five miles for an hour of non-productive pushing, pulling, lifting, and climbing, and drive back. At home I would step out of the car and wave to Adam as he hefted hay bales into one of the barns. He would wave back with a beautifully toned arm; he does the old-fashioned circuit: manual labor. But Adam actually needed biceps; I didn't. I had somehow accepted the idea that I should look as if I regularly tossed fifty-pound hay bales, when actually the chief exertion of my day was strapping on my bra—unless a pen rolled off my desk and I had to lean over the arms of my office chair to grope about and grab it. I needed only my brain and its packaging to do my job.

My whole life I wanted to be beautiful, but I never particularly did anything about it, not from unconsciousness of my looks, I'm sorry to say, but from vanity of character. I was proud not to own a hair dryer or shave my legs or have a clue how to put on lipstick, and the benefits of feeling superior to all those women who wasted time and money and mental energy on their appearance far outweighed in my mind the possible benefits of my spending *any* time or money on it. Even when I occasionally tried to slim down, I did it surreptitiously. I didn't join Weight Watchers or a Jazzercise class; I didn't stand in the check-out line with appetite suppressants or fitness magazines or anything else that might have marked me as a dieter. I exercised in the privacy of my own home and changed the subject at dinner when someone remarked on how little I was eating. When I lost any weight, I acted as if I were pleasantly surprised. Unconcern for my appearance was the appearance I aimed to achieve.

Until the summer before my wedding. I didn't buy a hair dryer or a razor and Adam had vowed not to marry me if I wore any makeup, but, in an effort to look more beautiful, more bridal, more like the way I felt I was supposed to look on my wedding day, I did something I never dreamed I would do: I joined Gold's Gym.

In Jewish tradition the bride undergoes purification before her wedding day with a dip in the *mikveh*, the ritual bath. It is a ritual of cleansing and rebirth that she will, theoretically, repeat throughout her married life to purify herself after menstruation, about which Judaism is quite superstitious. My sister Amy did it, though for her it was a one-time event, a preparation for marriage. Gathered in Virginia a week before her wedding (three years before mine), we—one bride, two sisters, one mom, one friend—went down to the south fork of the Shenandoah River and gamely waded into the cold and swirling water. Amy went all the way in; having scampered back up the bank as soon as our thighs were wet, the rest of us were waiting for her with towels when she came out. I enjoyed the whole thing the way you enjoy indulging someone when they have a right to be indulged, the way you enjoy bringing someone breakfast in bed on her birthday. Anything Amy wants, she gets. I couldn't really understand, though, why she wanted to do it, what meaning she found in this male religion's ritual response to fears of female impurity.

Her urge for premarital purification is quite common, though. Marriage isn't just a moment at which one is the conscious center of attention. It is a critical rite of passage, a major transition in life, however symbolic rather than substantive that transition may be. And people throughout the world have ways of readying themselves for that rite. The Hindu religion has a complicated ritual of *sagun*, in which, among other things, the bride visits the family shrine and is anointed with vermilion and turmeric. Moroccans believe they must remove evil spirits called *bas* from the bride and groom, for which they bathe them, paint them with henna, make loud noises, sing, and pray. Then, three days before the wedding, seven buckets of lukewarm water are poured over the bride by seven women. Water seeps into many prewedding purification rituals: brides in ancient Greece bathed in pure spring water and tossed in a few coins to placate the water spirits; Zulu brides bathe with their female companions on the wedding morning; in Finland they visit a sauna; in some parts of India the bride's relatives proceed to the nearest river, where they ask the water goddesses to bless the water they will carry home in jars to wash the bride.

Fasting is another means of ritual purification. Among the G'wi bushmen of Botswana, the bride fasts silently and without moving for four days; bride and groom are then both washed, their heads are shaved, and they are tattooed. A Jewish tradition is for both the bride and groom to fast on the day of the wedding, breaking the fast only after the wedding ceremony when they are in seclusion (*yichud*) together. They are cleansed, and then they symbolically begin their new life as a married couple when they eat their first meal together alone. I thought this was a lovely idea, but Adam and I didn't do it; my blood sugar is too temperamental to combine fasting with walking down an aisle. And Adam wasn't going to truck with that kind of foolishness: after all, a bagel brunch was being given in our honor that morning, and the bagel brunch is the Jewish law that supersedes all others.

But I think my gym-joining, and my fiber cereal, nonfat yogurt, and salad diet came from this same urge toward purification. I wanted to go through my wedding pure, purged of fat, clean, transformed. The *Encyclopedia of Religion* calls self-denial "an act of purification for laymen." My whole summer was a prolonged fast, a continued effort to change myself, to atone for past physical sins—not sexual ones, just sloth and gluttony—and past mental ones. And the pain I put myself through in the gym might well have been a modern, secular form of the mortification of the flesh that characterizes other purification rituals. I had had lapses in determination and focus, and I was going to change that. Plus look good in my wedding photos. But that was part of the same impulse: to marry as a new and perfect person.

The purifying in all of these cultures isn't so much an aim in itself as an attempt to return to an earlier, purer state. It is an attempt at rebirth. It's no accident that water is by far the most popular form of purification; the ceremonies ritually enact a return to the womb, the primordial self. As Anita Diamant, author of *The New Jewish Wedding*, says when discussing the mikveh, "immersion creates newborns." And branding, tattooing, and head-shaving are all ritual ways to mark the "birth" of a new being.

In the modern, secular West, we have our own ways of making our bodies new as we enter the married state. Among the ads for photographers and wedding consultants in a wedding issue of the *San Francisco Examiner Magazine*, there are ads for personal trainers ("Six Week ReShaping Program") and cosmetic dentists ("The Secret of Her Smile? Invisible Braces"). There's even one, above the ad of a matchmaking service and next to that of a furniture store, for the Cosmetic Laser Surgery Center, with the tag line, "A New You . . ." I doubt many brides go as far as collagen treatments and liposuction, but I do know the tendency to join a gym with nine or six or three months to go before the wedding is widespread; membership directors in gyms say "absolutely" an impending wedding is "top of the list" of reasons people give for signing up. Prewedding dieting is also rampant and practically requisite: the *Modern Bride* website has a prominent link on its opening page to NutriSystem.com. Certainly I've been to weddings where the bride has remade herself to the point that she can barely be recognized, where women I've never seen in lipstick appear painted like dolls, with red circles on their cheeks and blue-dusted eyelids. They want to make themselves look like brides.

A *Bride's* magazine article on hairdressing asks a stylist at Frédéric Fekkai Beauté de Provence to name the most common bridal hair mistake. The answer: "picking a totally different style for the wedding day." According to him, brides go a little too far in their drive to be renewed; rather than trying to be a new woman, she should try for a "more graceful, glamorous version of her everyday self." Of course this is sheer hypocrisy on the part of the magazine: it and its hefty competitors promote anything but the idea that you the bride are just you dressed up for a nice party. Your everyday self probably wouldn't go for tulle, an eight-foot train, a dress you can wear only once. Your everyday self wouldn't, for that matter, buy a five-dollar, 576-page magazine with 43 pages of cheerful prose and 533 pages of advertisements. We're not really talking about your everyday self, are we? A few of the 43 pages of prose might be, but the 533 pages of ads do just the opposite: they aggressively promote the concept of a new you.

It's not just the bride's looks the magazines encourage her to transform in preparation for becoming a wife. It's the whole person. Modern brides seem to want to be wed in such a different state of being that they require instruction manuals with articles on "Six Surefire Ways to Win Over His Family" and "Dance Fever—Getting Four Left Feet to Do Things Right." Wedding etiquette books, with their lists of instructions, their do's and don'ts, implicitly support a vast commercial network that includes dance lessons and tuxedo rentals, but they also support the engaged person's determination to be a new person. To be the sort of person who writes thank-you notes in black or blue-black ink, who employs tact when dealing with relatives, who tips appropriately, who can graciously accept a toast made in her honor. You're thirty-three and you don't know how to mingle? Fine for a single person, but if you're going to be a bride, you need to read this article on Making the Rounds: 10 Do's and Don'ts.

One ad for Waterford crystal does admit that there might be a difference between the old you and the bride you. It shows a woman in baggy pants, sneakers, an undershirt, and an enormous bridal veil, laughing as she looks at herself in the mirror. No, purrs the ad, the traditional image of the bride doesn't seem like you—and neither does buying crystal stemware—but that's part of the fun, isn't it? Becoming a new person is part of the magic, the Cinderella joy, of getting married.

Whatever else we might do to prepare ourselves for our weddings, the vast majority of us in the West wear white for the day itself. In *Tried and Trusseau*, Jennifer Rogers calls the white wedding dress "the baptismal garment that clothes you during your transition from a previous existence to a new life." Chinese brides wear red, the color of happiness; Spanish peasant brides and Icelandic brides wear black; Indonesian royalty wear gold; and so on. But in the West, the white wedding dress is almost ubiquitous, perhaps because so many of our other rituals of purity and rebirth have been lost or forgotten. White has been Westerners' preferred wedding dress color since the Victorian era. We know that the color white first signified simply wealth, since a white dress could hardly be one's only dress, and therefore wearing one showed you could afford others, as well as the means to keep it clean. But as clothes got cheaper, white lost its connotation of wealth. Then all it took to have a clean white dress was effort; which was, theoretically, all it took to keep oneself "clean" sexually—the virginity metaphor was an easy leap. Even if you shrink from the notion that purity should be equated with virginity, the color white is still, in our bleached modern world, the color of clean, the color of new. The color of a T-shirt before it grows sweat stains, the color of paper before it's been inked, the color of snow before it's grimed with car exhaust. It's the color of before. Before you were married. Before you had sex. Before you picked up each other's dirty dishes. Before you fought over who had to return the videos. If you are marrying long *after* all that, draping yourself in white helps you recall that sense of before, of beginning. It helps you feel as if you're on the verge of a new life.

Almost all Western brides wear white. Many also wear veils, the very symbol of the bride. Even if she's wearing baggy pants and a T-shirt, a woman in a veil is identifiably a bride. Most of us wear dresses occasionally, but few of us ever wear hats, let alone veils. So when we wear one, it signifies wedding; *nubere*, in fact, is Latin both for veiling and for marrying. In Roman times, after the terms of a wedding were set, the bride was veiled to signify that she had been purchased and could be unwrapped only by her new owner, her husband. Occasionally, this custom did not work toward the benefit of the husband: using a veil, Jacob's father-in-law tricked him into marrying Leah rather than Rachel, whose hand in marriage he had worked seven years to earn. Whether the power belonged to her father or to her husband-to-be, the creature under the veil had no power at all; her vision was blurred if not blinded, which meant she had to be led down the aisle. Today veils in the East imply modesty, humility, and subservience to men, and veils in the West carry (if only subliminally) those implications as well. More than anything, though, the veil marks the marginal state between unmarried and married. No male eyes, particularly not the groom's, are supposed to see the face of the bride before the ceremony; according to one etiquette book, "people thought that if the groom saw the bride before the ceremony, she would not be pure and new." In fact, even the bride isn't supposed to look at herself. The veil, then, writes Peter Lacey in *The Wedding*, "serves as a kind of gift wrapping, a guarantee of newness." Behind the veil, the magic is worked that transforms a woman from the old self to the new: after the word "wife" is pronounced, the veil is lifted. *Voilà*.

But what about the groom? When and how does his transformation take place? Men don't appear to have the same urge to transform themselves for their weddings. I think it crossed Adam's mind that it was nice to be marrying at the end of the hay season, at his most buff and brown and trim, but I suspect that if we had married in May instead, he wouldn't have lifted weights or lain in a tanning booth. His wedding costume would be much less revealing than mine, and his body consciousness was about a tenth of mine, and in these respects he probably resembled the average American groom. So is it simply that his transformation wasn't physical? I don't think so: worldwide, though some premarital rituals include the groom, most are aimed specifically at the bride. And here in America, almost all the advice books, advertising, and guides to prewedding preparation are aimed at her. The male bachelor party can be seen as a rite of purgation: one last expulsion of the evil spirits that inhabit the single man, in preparation for marrying. But that's almost all a man goes through on the official American journey to becoming a husband.

Men feel less driven to transform and purify themselves simply because our culture does not call upon them to become new people when they marry. Traditionally, the woman moves from her parents' house to her husband's, the woman takes her husband's name, the woman becomes a "wife" whereas the man remains a "man"—as in the phrase, "man and wife." "Mr." remains "Mr."; "Miss" becomes "Mrs."

The new person a wedding creates in our culture is the wife, not the husband. And it has been that way throughout history: women in ancient Greece figured their age from their marriage day, not their birth. Sociologist Marcia Seligson wrote, "While little boys are dreaming heroic dreams of conquering worlds, little girls are yearning for transformation—becoming beautiful, becoming a woman, becoming a mommy . . . marriage is the single event which will presumably guarantee that metamorphosis." She wrote that in the 1970s, but there's no getting around the fact that, even today, it is the bride who wears white, the bride who wears the veil, the bride who takes the ritual bath. It is the bride who is transformed into someone else when the minister turns the couple around and presents to his congregation "Mr. and Mrs. (Groom's Name Here)."

When I was in junior high, I practiced writing out my name with various boys' names at the end of it: Kate Whitmore, Kate Shirkey, Kate Showalter. But that was it for the idea of changing my name. Maybe it was my growing interest in and respect for words, but I began to believe that the fact that women are identified by their husbands' names *must* affect our perception of their individuality, their importance, their independence. Their identity. Whitmore, Shirkey, Showalter, the names of my junior high crushes, are all common names in the Shenandoah Valley, where I grew up—they are the names that fill the phonebooks and the cemeteries. They make me homesick with their geographic specificity. Indeed, Travis, Lee, and Phillip were all from families whose local roots dug down for generations. My family had lived in the area for only ten years. If I had taken one of those boys' names, I would have taken on that local identity as well; and though I have no objection to that old Valley heritage, neither do I have a real connection to it. Whitmore, Shirkey, or Showalter, as my last name, would have described me only as much as it described my husband. A friend of mine, having exchanged her birth name, Golden, for her husband's Oppenneer, noted how odd it was that "nobody can tell anything about me from my name." Her background is Jewish; her new name is Dutch.

How can my name not describe me better than Adam's? In an article on whether women should change their names when they marry, Texas pastor Bishop Thomas Jakes, Sr., makes a common argument: "Some women think that they lose their identity by taking their husbands' name, but that seems futile because she's born into her father's name. She moves from one man's name to another. But her name doesn't give her identity; it's who she is and what she does that determines her destiny." That's true, of course. But Adam was born into his father's name, too; if I have to go by someone's father's name, I'd rather go by my father's, as I have my whole life. And since, as the bishop argues, names don't matter anyway, since they don't carry identity or make destiny, men should be equally willing to change theirs. Right? Wrong: "When you get married, the man's name is supposed to go on. That's the way God designed it," according to singer Angie Winans (interviewed for this same article). "We are supposed to carry his name. The Bible says when you marry you become one. You become one, and it's not about changing your identity; love overlooks all of that."

I like the idea of a merged identity; on some level that's what a wedding is: two people declaring that their connection, their commitment to one another, has fundamentally changed them, has changed them for life. I like the idea of starting anew, becoming a new person. Before I married, I did wish that something would change on August 31, 1997, that some sign would make clear to the world that Adam had become part of me and vice versa. "This time three months from now, I'll be . . . ," I thought, and was a little disappointed to have to say, Ms. Kate Cohen, because that was the same old, single me. But Mrs. Adam Greenberg was too much not me. It would be lovely to have a little change, one that felt appropriate. Greenberg isn't him, it's his family—Adam was what I was officially declaring to be a part of me. I should be Kate Adam Cohen and he should be Adam Kate Greenberg. That would be about right.

But sharing a single last name is appealing too, since it creates, by naming, a single family unit. I like being able to say to Adam, "Let's have the Mendels over" or "The Shers invited us for dinner." Yes, the Shers are Nina and Aaron and Ben and Jackie, they are individuals, but they are also as a family a single force in our lives, and I enjoy referring to them that way. And it's a lot easier than saying, "Do you think Gary and Lissa and Maggie and Sarah will come?" which we do because Lissa appended her last name to Gary's with a hyphen, but Gary and their daughters have her birth name as their middle name and his name as their last.

I would prefer it if Adam and I had the same last name, if our family had a family name. I even like the idea of sacrificing individual identity to make a single family identity. And I don't think I'm unable or unwilling to make that kind of sacrifice. It's the unfairness of the system that stops me, the fact that the sacrifice is expected to be mine, because I am the woman. If it switched back and forth: if, during odd years, women changed their names and during even ones, men changed theirs, that would be fine. Or if the shorter name prevailed, or the less common name. Or if a panel of judges were to decide, as part of the engagement process, which name sounded better: first you get your marriage license, then you order your invitations, then you go up before the Board of Appellative Aesthetics. But that's not how it is. When I tell people my brother-in-law took my sister's name, they act shocked, and a little disturbed by what they assume to be an act of subservience—as if I had told them he wears a leash.

Because, though Jakes and Winans talk about the name change as a merger of identities, what they really mean is a corporate takeover. Winans doesn't even pause before making the leap between "you become one" and "we are supposed to carry his name," between the idea that men and women should have a single identity and the idea that, to do so, women should give theirs up. For most people the one idea naturally follows the other. Eighteenth-century British legal scholar William Blackstone spelled it out: "In marriage, husband and wife are one person and that person is the husband."

Tracing this system back to its roots is a simple matter: open your Bible. The enormous influence that book has on us all is illustrated by the fact that I can say, "open your Bible," and chances are you've got one, or at least have heard of it, no matter what you may think of its contents. We don't have to read very far, it turns out: "and the rib which the Lord God has taken from the man he made into a woman and brought her to the man. Then the man said, 'This at last is bone of my bones and flesh of my flesh.'"

The Koran tells Muslims that God "hath created you of one man and of him created his wife." Judaism, of course, shares with Christianity the story of Adam's rib. And Orthodox Judaism, even as practiced in the 1990s in upstate New York, hadn't moved far from such a vision of woman as an appendage of a man. Soon after we were married, we received an invitation to join the local Orthodox synagogue (to which Adam's father belongs). The membership form opened like a book, the left side of which was headed "Member" and the right side of which was headed "Member's Wife." It might as well have said "Member's Rib."

You don't have to do anything to keep your birth name,

you don't have to go to City Hall, or fill out any forms. So it didn't really occur to me until after I married, when everyone from the neighbors to close relatives started to call me Greenberg, to consider the choice I had made, and to wonder just how many women make the same one. Not many, it turns out. A full 90 percent of U.S. women adopt their husband's name. Of the 10 percent who don't, 5 percent hyphenate (and many women I know who hyphenate do so unilaterally—the man keeps the name he grew up with), and 3 percent choose other options, such as "Hillary Rodham Clinton." Only 2 percent do what probably 99.99 percent of all men do: keep their birth names.

When hay dealers call, or salesmen, or the bank, they make the statistically correct assumption that I took my husband's name. Even knowing to expect them, I routinely fumble these calls: I say "Hello?" and they say, "Mrs. Greenberg?" and I say "Um, no, but this is Adam Greenberg's wife." Then there's a pause, and I add: "We have different last names." And I get that funny feeling you get when you've explained too much of yourself to strangers. I'm not annoyed that they call me Mrs. Greenberg, and I don't feel particularly called upon to open their eyes to the possibility of a husband and wife with different surnames; I just can't answer to Adam's mother's name. How long, I wonder, did it take her to answer to it?

A young Orthodox Jewish wife I met not long after marrying asked me why I decided not to take my husband's name. I think she's the only person who's ever actually asked me why, and I liked her for that. I said that it never really occurred to me to *change* my name. She said she still used her maiden name sometimes for business purposes, and her husband gets angry about it. "He says, 'That person doesn't exist anymore.'" The bride, pained, confided, "She does exist, she's still in me."

Purification rituals come in many forms, including bathing

and fasting and mortification of the flesh. Another common form is substitution, in which one transfers the pollutants of one's soul or body to an object, an animal, or a human scapegoat. The object would then be discarded or burned, the animal sacrificed, the human driven from the community. In the fairly rigid patriarchy of Jewish Orthodoxy, a single female is a dangerous thing; the danger that inhabits her—potential independence, potentially unharnessed sexuality—can be ritually cast off along with the birth name. When the birth name is exorcised, so is (ritually at least) all that's unclean and threatening about the single female. Because she hung onto her birth name, this young Orthodox bride acted as if she were hanging on to guilt and sin. But all she was clutching was a vestige of her unmarried self.

I think she was probably clutching because her husband and her religion wanted her to let go; as their grip tightened, hers did too. Maybe women who don't feel constrained to do it take pleasure in casting off their old selves; they might see the new name as an opportunity to start new that men never get. Women can pack into that birth name all their flaws and their childishness and the scenes from their past that they can barely recall without wincing from the shame. These can belong to the old self, the one that disappeared once the veil was lifted. "It's a new life," one friend who changed her name told me. "I think it's appropriate to feel like a new person." And my friend born Golden said part of the reason she didn't mind changing her name was that "becoming married was like becoming a new person" and she welcomed that change, that new identity. Perhaps she could imagine, as her minister pronounced her new name, as her friends and relatives addressed her as often as possible as Mrs. Oppenneer just to give her a taste of the change, that she was embarking on a new life with new hope for the future.

But does she have a new life? Does she leave her old, imperfect self behind? However much we may try to toss away our old selves, few of us can be surprised when it doesn't work. Perhaps orthodox religions, perhaps even tame secular patriarchies like our own can reassure themselves that the volatile female has been cast away with her name, but has she? Does the community really escape its sin when it sacrifices the goat? It probably doesn't take long for a wife with a new name to discover that most of what she is is what she was before, that she still says things she regrets and she still fights with the man she loves and she still prefers sleeping late to keeping house. There's something sad in that discovery, but something powerfully good about it too: that the change in her name does not change her inner self, that there is an identity that transcends name and marital status. That she did not, in fact, substitute or purify her self away.

On the day that the dress fittings and the haircut and the bench presses were all leading to, on our wedding day, I didn't really look in a mirror. I brushed and parted my hair in the bathroom while I was still in my underwear, and then I never went back to check. I never looked at myself as a bride, never thought, There she is. And I think that's because, deep down, I knew she wasn't. I had wanted a new and better me. I wanted what those bridal magazines had promised. I wanted for this day, for this transition from the old life to the new, all of a sudden to be slim-hipped and lithe-limbed. To strip off the old body, the body I'd lived with, fought with my whole life, the body I used to undress in the dark when I first slept with Adam because I didn't want him to see it. I wanted a new one. And after three months of hard work, fierce concentration, and practically no cheating, I deserved a new one. After three months of air-conditioned sweat and self-consciousness, I got biceps, triceps, and a few ceps I can't even name. I gained the ability to do far more push-ups than I ever imagined, and even a chin-up. But I didn't end up with the perfect body; I ended up with *my* body, the same one I had before, with more muscle and less fat. Slope-shouldered, short-waisted, wide-hipped, thigh-flabby, and ankle-heavy. Me.

The mikveh is a physical bath for a spiritual cleansing—you're supposed to be physically clean already when you climb in. My purification at the gym, though I'd thought it was physical, was really spiritual instead. When I met Adam, since my body wasn't what I wanted, I wanted to be bodiless. He set out to convince me, first, that I had a body, and second, that my body was fine. He did not try to convince me that it was stunning or perfect, just that it was fine. And with his help, with his refusal either to mock or to overpraise my body, I was convinced. But still, secretly, I had wanted not a fine body, but a perfect body; still, secretly, I had believed that I could have it.

The summer before my wedding I learned for certain that I couldn't. That was my mikveh. What I washed away with all that sweat wasn't my body's imperfections; it was the illusion I had clung to that I could be, would ever be, not me. I had long ago internalized the pressure to look a certain way; I had been resisting that pressure within myself for years. But for my wedding I wanted to be new, I wanted to start over. So I gave in to the pressure that summer, dove into it. And when I came out, my body had barely changed at all, and I knew, finally, that it never would. Come August I would walk down the aisle not as the perfect woman, but as myself. A little disappointed by that, a little relieved, and a little wiser. Without a veil and without makeup. In a body that was more me than my own name.

6

Portrait of the Bride and Groom

We decided to have some photographs taken of our wedding. That sentence sounds reasonable enough, but it is manifestly false. We didn't "decide" to have wedding photographs; we considered the question for about as long as we considered whether we would bathe the day of our wedding. Would we invite our parents, would we dress up, would we feed our guests—all of these deliberations, given enough context, you might take seriously. But would we record the event? The answer was instamatic. Photography is a crucial American wedding rite, second only (and only barely) to the vows.

And taking the wedding photographs takes longer than saying the vows. You can't think of a wedding you attended that wasn't photographed, I'm certain, but can you think of many in which there was no time *scheduled* for photographs? Cameras are certainly advanced to the point that we don't have to sit still for them, and photographers are perfectly capable of following us around and recording the event. Still we structure our weddings around posed portraits, either dressing two hours early or making the reception start late in order to have our pictures taken. Even when a wedding is reduced to its barest elements, photographs are among them. When our friends got married in the chambers of a judge, Adam and I, their witnesses, snapped photos the entire time that we weren't bent over to sign the marriage license. Dozens of photographs record the ten-minute ceremony.

Photography was invented in 1839; in its first thirty years, wedding portraits were relatively rare. Painfully long exposure times and great expense may have deterred couples from having a daguerreotype made, but novelty was the more likely bar. A wedding was a solemn, traditional thing, and photography, like much new technology, was at first a sort of magic trick, a crowd-goggler. From the 1870s wedding portraits became more and more common. Photographers would bring their equipment to the homes of the wealthy; the less wealthy would go to the local studio to have their portraits done while in their wedding finery. These were direct, frontal shots, occasionally varied by the classic pose of the demure bride, eyes downcast. They were, in other words, oil paintings the middle class could afford. In the late 1880s, photographers were making more informal portraits in and around the home on the day of the wedding, and by 1900, photographs of celebrity weddings were regularly being reproduced in newspapers and magazines. Amateur photography spread in the 1930s with improvements in the 35mm camera. But wedding pictures continued more or less to imitate painted portraiture, until about 1940, when, with the Speed Graphic camera, wedding photographers could act like press photographers and follow the events as they occurred. Thus began what Barbara Norfleet, curator of the photography collection at Harvard, calls the prolific age of wedding photography: an age in which people started to keep wedding albums as such, and the studio photographer began to make his living primarily from wedding photos.

Today, the professionals aren't the only ones taking pictures. So are the guests with their own point-and-shoots, and the guests who volunteer to take charge of the disposable cameras placed at each table, and the children who manage to get hold of those cameras by the end of the reception, so as to provide the newlyweds with blurry closeups of other children's tongues. Weddings today produce miles of film, and now miles of videotape as well. Odds are good that if the family hires but one photographer ever, it is a wedding photographer; if the bookshelf in the den holds only one photo album, it is a wedding album; if the mantelpiece boasts only one framed photograph, it is a wedding photograph.

I don't remember being fixated as a child on my future wedding; I daydreamed more of deathless fame than of domestic bliss. But I did take pleasure in studying my parents' wedding album. Their images in those photographs were lovely to me, but faintly alien, as if they were creatures in a larval stage. At wedding age, twenty-one, my parents looked the same as they did at, say, thirty-one (when I was seven), but more naked, more coiffed and shorn (the difference in style between 1967 and 1977), scrubbed clean of worry lines, and more delicate, with skin so free of blemish I wanted to reach out to protect it from sun and time.

They looked young and they looked like movie stars, the other people we are accustomed to seeing as the dewy-eyed core of a carefully costumed cast. Wedding photographers think of themselves as directors, and describe their client brides and grooms as "stars for a day"; they reach over to the groom/leading man to turn his chin in just the right way to catch the light. In the wedding photo we carry in our heads before we marry, in which we play bride or groom, the face in the space next to us is frequently the blurry composite of what our father or mother looked like in wedding finery and what some celebrity would. In my parents' photo album, my father was a handsome, dark-haired man in a morning coat; surely at age seven I pictured some version of him as my groom. Other imaginary grooms flickered and winked at me from movie screens. When I was eight, nine, ten, I had a crush on the young Frank Sinatra from *On the Town*, and one as well on Tony Perkins (pre-*Psycho* and practically adolescent) in *Friendly Persuasion*, and on Gary Cooper in *Mr. Deeds Goes to Town*. I liked the vulnerable ones: the innocent, the pacifist, the bumpkin. I admired Cary Grant and Fred Astaire too, in a more distant way; they were so sophisticated, I couldn't really imagine them in love with me, no matter how I pined for them. I had no interest at all, though, in Clark Gable or Humphrey Bogart—tough guys—or in Gene Kelly, more handsome than Fred Astaire, I admit, but too brashly self-assured and self-loving. I preferred the slyly hopeful hangdog tilt of Astaire's wedge-shaped head.

Around the same time in his life, Adam was watching more TV than movies; he had his heart set on Lynda Carter as Wonder Woman and on Lindsay Wagner as the Bionic Woman. Women of action. Wonder Woman was also a woman of cleavage, to be sure, with an hourglass figure as cartoonish as the comic from which she spun, but you can't say the Bionic Woman was a blow-up doll. She was just cool. As he got older, Adam gravitated less to women who could smash through bolted doors, but he still hankered after the strong ones: Carrie Fisher as Princess Leia in *Star Wars*, and later, tomboys played by Mary Stuart Masterson. I moved on to foreign-born sufferers and intellectuals—Mel Gibson, not in *The Road Warrior* but in *Gallipoli* and *The Year of Living*

Dangerously; Anthony Andrews playing Sebastian Flyte in
Brideshead Revisited.

When we spoke to the man who would be our wedding
photographer, we talked about how much time we would
give over to the photographs on our wedding day, we stressed
our desire for black-and-white pictures, we promised a list
of the portraits we wanted. It hit me as we talked that the
image of the groom in that archetypal wedding photo in
my head was soon going to be fixed. Permanently. Permanently not Frankie or Tony or Gary. Permanently not my high
school boyfriend or my college crushes. The blurry image—
the blur of a lifetime of men in tuxes superimposed upon one
another—would snap into focus, snap permanently into
Adam. In hundreds of pictures for our children and their children to pore over.

But why hundreds? Why are photographs so important to
us, to all of us? Weddings have always been at least partly for
show, a demonstration of the wealth, generosity, prestige, or
piety of those (or the parents of those) who wed. They are a
form of social display, the face we present to the world. As
such they are the perfect subjects for photographs, which
can make a temporary social display permanent. With photographs, writes sociologist Erving Goffman, "The individual
is able to catch himself at a moment . . . when what is visible
about him attests to social matters about which he is proud.
A moment, in short, when he is in social bloom, ready, therefore, to accept his appearance as a typification of himself."
More simply, as one photographer told sociologist Charles
Lewis, "The photographs prove they had their day."

Photographs have been able to achieve these ends since
the medium was invented, but never before have they been
such a vital part of the proceedings. Getting married is
unthinkable today without photographs, partly, I believe,
because display is more and more crucial to getting married.

Weddings are becoming less practical, less consequential, and more expressive. When the bride and groom have lived together, made friends together, and merged families and finances, wedding doesn't so much make a union as it portrays one. Like a photograph. So taking photographs of the wedding—recording the display, getting "proof"—is natural, even necessary, at a modern wedding.

Photographs and weddings are similar in another way too: they stop time. They allow you to turn around and look at yourself, who you are, what you look like, who's beside you at this moment. They make a before and after in a life where changes are so gradual that the years merge into one another without mercy. I can't tell you much about myself in the moment when Adam and I met; I can't imagine what we talked about. Who we are now, how we behave to each other now distorts my memory of who we were then; looking back, I am always in my own way. I could weep with the frustration of it, a cat chasing her tail, a child trying to shed his shadow. Maybe I could retrieve those first few months, dodge my now-self and catch for a second the then-me, if I knew exactly what I looked like then, what Adam was wearing, what songs we were listening to, who I considered to be my closest friends, what balance of affection and competition I felt for my sisters. All of this is what a wedding does; it is a snapshot in time, a record of who you are, whom you love, what you value, what you believe.

Barbara Norfleet says that wedding photographs "may be the best [record] we have of the historical changes in fashion, expressions, gestures and manners; and the variations which derive from income, religion, sex and ethnicity." A practiced eye reading the photographs in her book could glean much from the cut of a lapel, the sheen in a man's hair, how a woman carries her purse. It's tempting to think that if we just had enough photographs, we could somehow hold

on to who we were at a certain point in time, that our physical reality, if read carefully enough, held all the clues to our
inner selves as well. Picture this: a bride of twenty-seven, a
groom of twenty-nine, though they both look young for their
years. Healthy, clean when not working, they smile often. Do
they look Jewish? Maybe not the first thing that would spring
to mind, but it wouldn't surprise someone either. Beyond
that, who can say the little calculations that people make,
the instant information they gather? Anytime I left the house
with dirty hair the summer we got married, I wore the only
baseball cap I had that fit me right: tan-colored with an
AIDS ribbon embroidered on it. It felt like wearing a bumper
sticker on my head. But you don't need a bumper sticker to
deduce something about the driver of, say, a spanking clean
sport utility vehicle: with or without an AIDS awareness hat,
I didn't go around incognita. You could have figured out
quite a bit from my unshaved legs and unmade face, my cotton shorts, cotton T-shirt, and sandals on a weekday afternoon. Maybe someone accustomed to reading that complex
code of clothes and coloring and gesture could have looked
at Adam and me and deduced that both our parents' marriages were intact, that we both had siblings (two sisters for
me, two brothers and a sister for him), that we were for
gun control and against capital punishment, that we had
gotten good, expensive educations, that we loved to go to the
movies. That we were beginning to fear losing our young
selves, losing hold of what we once were, or thought we
were. That we wanted to marry, to frame a portrait of ourselves for others—and for ourselves—to see.

I'll start at the top, since that's where you would start if you
were looking at us. At the top, we start at about the same
place. Adam would argue that he's taller than I, and maybe

when you line us up back to back, he is, but if you have to line us up back to back . . . well, I think I've made my point. About five foot five. I love that I look right in his eyes when I dance with him, but walking arm-in-arm is kind of a pain—one person's shoulder should be a little higher than the other's for it to work. Hugs work, and holding hands.

But I'm starting at the top. Adam has thick, sandy-brown hair that goes blond after a summer of farmwork. It is thinning from the front, though not evenly; there's a peninsula in the center that's in danger of becoming an island. He doesn't like his growing baldness, but dislikes more the idea of trying to hide it, so he was planning to cut it close, even crew-cut it, after the wedding. My hair is brown and soft and straight and thin. For years I tried to make it thick and curly (with perms, curlers, a mass of tiny braids), then I hid it in a bun, then I finally realized it had to be short. It was about chin length, that summer, longer in the front than the back, parted on the side.

Adam's eyes are set very deep, so you get drawn into his face when you look at him, drawn to his gold-brown lashes and to the eyes themselves, hazel or green depending on the day and the color of his shirt. I'm not sure if eyes can look thoughtful or intelligent—maybe these are qualities we assign them after we know the mind behind them—but if they can, his do. He lets them rest, at length, on the person to whom he is speaking. Unless he happens to be watching a baseball game. When he gets excited at a deliciously tense moment during a game or a movie, he presses the backs of his hands against his closed eyes and wriggles his fingers. I have no idea why. My eyes are large and brown and long-lashed. I have thick brows, which I consider my best feature. I close my eyes during the gruesome parts of movies and *X-Files* episodes; I see no reason to store those images in my brain. Then I have to ask Adam to tell me what happened.

When he's feeling generous, he spares me the goriest details.

Adam's nose is rather delicate; he gets it from his mother, who is of Scotch/Welsh descent. When he plays hockey on his parents' pond, the tip of his nose goes red. The tip of my nose goes numb when I drink two glasses of wine. The tip is pretty much all there is, too, because my nose is tiny, too small for my face. When Adam and my father were putting a photo album together before our wedding, they had a black-and-white picture they wanted to use of me with two college friends, but when they enlarged it, my nose actually didn't show up. They had to ask my brother-in-law, an artist, to draw it in. Mine is the nose that rules in this house, though: Adam tosses me his day-old shirts to sniff the armpits and deliver judgment—Can I wear this?

His hearing is the hearing that rules. He claims his is much better than mine (his actual words are, "Oh, I forgot, you can't hear"), but I think that's mostly because he mutters responses to me without looking up and because, from years of reading on the sofa next to someone watching televised sports, I've learned to tune out what doesn't interest me. It's true, however, that I don't hear the cat when he cries to get in at night, and I don't hear the phone when I'm sitting on the porch. What I do hear, though, I remember: I have a good aural memory, which records conversations word for word. Adam doesn't, and whenever he tells a funny line from a movie wrong, it makes me crazy. It makes him crazy when I correct him. He believes humor lies in concept and I believe it lies in the particulars, in words and rhythm. The different values we accord the general and the specific cause us problems in arguments, too: he thinks I use distinctions as a way to dither; I think he willfully mishears or misrepresents. What he mishears with are nice, tidy ears; mine stick out a little.

He has a beautiful mouth, small and kissable, with full

lips; the bottom one can fairly be described as succulent. Straight teeth. My teeth are crooked and darkened with fillings, but I have good lips, too, with plenty of color. He craves the taste of sugar; I crave salt and fat. I also crave food generally, in a way he doesn't understand; some days it seems to me that I devote most of my time and energy to a combination of snacking and snack-resistance. Partly because of this greater interest in food, my tastebuds, like my olfactory glands, take precedence: I'm the one who has to nibble the turkey to see if it's gone bad, to identify the herb that suffuses a restaurant soup.

The skin of my face is soft and nearly always clear; you can tell when I'm under unusual stress, because I will have a lone pimple. The weekend Adam's mom threw me a bridal shower, I had a lone pimple on my right cheek. These rare blemishes drive me crazy; I take my clear skin for granted. The vanity I like to pretend I don't have drags me to the mirror every forty-five minutes for a zit update. Adam's skin is nearly always clear, but it is rarely clean-shaven. His beard grows so fast that that clean, soft look, which makes his lips seem all the redder and his eyes all the greener, threatens to disappear the moment you see it. I get in as much nuzzling as possible in these few smooth moments, as long as I'm not angry with him. I don't want to touch him when I'm angry with him; it's not purposeful punishment, I just recoil, because his body seems somehow to embody whatever he did wrong. But he *loves* to touch me when I'm angry with him, as if the very fact of his arm around me should remind me that his wrong was slight, and that it's wrong of me now to slight him. See?—his hand implies as it rests on the back of my neck—*I've* forgiven *you* . . . Naturally this makes me angrier.

Adam has a strong neck, and his chest hair climbs up into that little nook below his Adam's apple. He likes to wear turtlenecks, and, though I've never liked the way they look on me, he has convinced me to wear them too, since I'm always cold. This small bit of sartorial persuasion pleases him; he cites it as evidence that he can talk me into anything.

Adam's chest and shoulders and arms are a marvel to me. They are so male, so muscular, with hairy but not beastly chest and forearms, with a small waist and delicate wrists to give him grace. I have described his as a miniature epitome of the male form; small, but perfectly proportioned. And I would watch in awe and envy those first times he dressed in front of me: boxers, jeans, T-shirt—the late-twentieth-century American uniform—a perfect fit. The denim didn't strain or sag, the cotton tee was snug through the shoulders and pecs and just loose enough below the ribs to suggest a slender waist. If there's a uniform that fits me, it's Renaissance Italian, something one of Botticelli's women would wear: high-waisted, defined around the breasts, but below that, all billow and drape. I've got delicate upper chest bones, small shoulders, large breasts, and a short torso. As female as he is male with an emphasis on breast and hip. Just not female in the way my culture wants me to be: buxom but somehow also narrow-hipped and free from body fat. Adam's body is far closer to the current Western ideal.

Adam's hands are always warm. His fingers are strong, a little stubby, and he gets calluses in the summer from handling hay bales. He bites his nails when we watch TV, and I reach over and push his hand away from his mouth without looking. His hands understand screwdrivers and wrenches and hay hooks and electric wires and joysticks and how long to hold down the VCR's fast-forward button to skip a commercial but not the first sentence of dialogue that follows. My hands understand bread dough and whisks and erasable colored pencils and wrapping paper and how much salt in the palm makes a teaspoon. I have small fingers, and tiny pinkies because the bones from the wrist to the knuckle on the outside of each hand are almost an inch shorter than they are supposed to be. I can't imagine punching anyone, partly because I am a conflict avoider (Adam is not), and partly because my baby pinkies give me a round and weak-looking fist.

He has a tight little butt. Where do people get these? He's not stair-stepping or working out to "Buns of Steel" videos. He just has this little round muscular thing, where I have wide and saggy. His is hairy, but that doesn't make up for it—I continue to resent him for his butt. And for the rest of the lower body: I've seen love handles come and go around that slim waist; random hairs mar the perfection of his broad back. But as far as I can tell, the strong, slim thighs, the precise knees, the sculptured calves, the tapered ankles, are unchanging and unchangeable. Gifts from God. The best you can say about these parts of *my* body is that they work. Which is, come to think of it, a lot: Adam tore a ligament in his right knee playing basketball in the winter before we married. And I had the shock of watching him—a man who doesn't understand why people walk since running was invented—lurch about on crutches. I, who don't understand why people play basketball since reading was invented, have never suffered such an injury. But I also have never gloried in such joy of body; I have never had speed or vertical leap, or good hands, or a quick pivot. When I listen to baseball announcers, I marvel at all the descriptions they use that will never be applied to me: Bob Costas will never say of me, "She's got an arm like a cannon," or "She gets out of the box in a hurry." My fastball will never have pop on it. I don't even know what having pop would feel like. But Adam does. All I can claim, in terms of athletic superiority, is a greater range of hip motion. When we tried to learn to rumba, Adam had a hard time with that scooping sideways hip movement; doing Latin dances, he always looked more like a wind-up toy than a person. American men rarely learn to isolate their hips.

And he is an American man, which still surprises me. After my crushes on Frankie and Tony and Gary, after my twenty-third viewing of *The Year of Living Dangerously*, after, in other words, I started to focus on men rather than movie stars, I didn't think I'd end up with an "American" man at all. I grew to picture myself alongside the skinny European type, healthy the way I'm healthy—with a body that works, holds him up over his desk, takes pleasure in walking down city streets—but not muscular, not athletic, not quite so *male*. I had thought I would marry the male version of me: someone whose body reflects his belief that life should consist primarily of reading, eating, talking, and drinking red wine. Not someone, in other words, who was recognizably American at all. But the life Adam's body is built for, or the life that has built Adam's body, includes sweaty team sports and days of manual labor so intense that he forgets to eat at all. An American life.

By virtue of his size, though, Adam does not have American feet. They are far too dainty: men's 6½. They have even, architectural tendons, soft skin, well-proportioned toes. He is quite proud of them, too, and will pull off sneakers and socks to challenge any comers in a foot beauty competition. It appears to be socially acceptable to brag about the beauty of one's feet, while the farther up the body, the more conceited one would have to be to brag. I have a nice face; sometimes, in candlelight, I think I have a lovely face. But I would never say that except in the midst of a confessional personal essay—and even then I would offer some kind of mitigating factor like candlelight. And yet, Adam can crow about his toes without risk of social disapproval, because feet are supposed to be ugly, or at least comical. Mine are comical indeed, with stubby, piggy toes, a square shape, and ankles so chunky I managed to get out of gym class once by claiming I'd twisted one: See, it's swelled up. Adam is reluctant, though, not only to brag about other parts of his body, but even to accept compliments for them. When I tell him he has beautiful eyes, he snorts and says, "That's what people say about people when they don't know how else to compliment them." But that's precisely what people say about me.

Beautiful feet and ugly feet can wear the same shoes. We're the same size. Perhaps that's the overriding impression bride- and groom-to-be gave as we stood side by side before we married: that we were the same size, a matched set. Or maybe the fact that our bodies more or less lined up with each other merely highlighted our contrasts, invited one to wonder instead at the vast differences contained within two humans, both about five foot five, both white, both weighing about as heavily on the earth.

Same frame, one could say of us, different pictures. One could say that too of wedding pictures; they are remarkably, relentlessly generic. The differences are in the details. You could probably name the shots in my parents' wedding album: the permutations and combinations of bride and groom, bride and groom with bride's family, bride and groom with groom's family; the cutting of the cake, the tossing of the bouquet, the throwing of the rice. Maybe this is because modern Western weddings are so remarkably similar to one another. But maybe the similarity of the photographs promotes the similarity of the weddings: the photographs we have seen, the images we carry in our heads, prompt us to structure our weddings the way we do. When we plan our weddings, we are re-creating, or at least reacting to, our parents' wedding albums, consciously or not. That's where we first saw what a wedding is, how a wedding day progresses, what a groom and a bride look like.

The first photographs in my parents' album are—guess!—of the bride and groom dressing for the wedding. In one photograph, my mom is surrounded by her mother and her maids of honor; they are fussing with her train and preparing to attach her veil. In another, my father is standing in his dark-grey morning coat as his father straightens his tie. Their families, these photographs imply, are more intimate with the bride and groom than bride and groom are with one another. With those images in my head I decided I wanted pictures of Adam and me dressing each other, as we often did for parties: he zips up my dress; I link his cuffs. In and of themselves these pictures would mean little; but in the wedding photograph genre they would be subversive in a way that satisfied my sense of self; they would show us to be long coupled and intimate, to be a family already.

It would never have occurred to me to take pictures of our dressing without those other, traditional, dressing pictures in my head. In fact, I didn't *really* need Adam's help to get dressed that day. Our friend Kathryn would be with us to do up my buttons if needed. And, to tell the truth, even in everyday life it's not a regular occurrence: occasionally he asks me if a shirt matches a pair of pants; occasionally I hand him a necklace to fasten. But it was important for me to show this, even if it wasn't strictly true on the day of the wedding, important for me to show the difference between our relationship as a marrying couple and my parents'.

But if I was staging this show for posterity, it was quite possible that they and their photographers had been too. After all, they had been dating for three years by the time they married; they had slept together and dressed together. In fact, though theirs are "dressing" photographs, there's no real dressing in them at all: no one's hitching up a slip, fumbling with a cummerbund, safety-pinning a bra strap under the sleeve of a dress. One photograph shows Grammy looking on in what appears to be an advisory capacity while my mom's older sister kneels at my sitting mother's feet, sliding a frilly blue garter over the bride's pantyhosed calf. A person actually dressing would normally put the garter on herself, *before* stepping into her dress. Mom has her dress neatly pulled up to the knee, with a hand on either side holding it in place, which would certainly get in the way were Aunt Jackie truly attempting to put the garter in its place mid-thigh. The photographs are, in short, entirely posed and discreet. They are fakes. As mine would be.

As, in a way, all wedding photographs are. These people have their arms around each other and are staring into the sun for no other reason than that someone is taking their photograph. That they are standing there at that moment may not be the only artifice, of course; *how* they are standing might be as well. As photographer Steve Sint says, "We show our subjects exactly how to sit, place their hands, tilt their heads, look at each other, and so on. We strive to have the resulting poses look perfectly natural, at ease, and bespeak of love and togetherness even though they may be very contrived and take several minutes to set up." That's for portraits. Portraits at least point to their own artificiality: we know that the moment caught on film is a moment *about* being caught on film, and nothing else, nothing "real."

But wedding photographers frequently stage more than just the portraits. Many books about wedding photography talk about a group of photographs called "altar returns," in which bride and groom and bridal party return to the altar to reenact, for the camera, the ceremony they have just performed. Altar returns are necessary, say the guides, because photographers are frequently prohibited from photographing the actual ceremony. The staging persists, how-ever, throughout the wedding events at which photos are permitted. Witness the checklists at the back of every wed-ding photography guide and in the pages of every bridal magazine, which include such theoretically spontaneous occurrences as Dad Helping Bride into Limousine, Bride and Groom Toasting Each Other, and Groom and Bride's Father Shaking Hands. Sint explains that to do their job properly, "all pros have to have some idea of what they're going to shoot." Fine—but they don't ask the bride and groom for a schedule of what's going to happen on the wedding day, cer-tainly not down to the level of who's shaking whose hand. Instead they have lists of expected shots written out in ad-vance. One wedding photography guidebook includes as an appendix a "Wedding Candid Checklist," which says it all, really. How can something pre-scripted be candid? Those checklists aren't just proof that all weddings are alike; they *make* all weddings alike, through the agency of the photog-rapher. "If the band leader forgets to invite the bride to dance with her father, the photographer must arrange it," advises another wedding photographer. "If, at the end of the reception, the bridal couple had not planned for a formal exit, the photographer may have to stage [it]." And so on.

So certain events occur in weddings because the photog-rapher expects them to, and because we, having looked at wedding albums all our lives, expect them to also. It's an unbreakable circle, and it encompasses more than simply what happens when. Photography guides suggest, in order to get some good "candid" shots, that the photographer have the maid of honor wink as she helps the bride adjust her garter, and that he instruct the best man to check his watch to imply the groom has only a few minutes of freedom left. They suggest telling the bride to lean over, kiss her father's cheek, and tell him she loves him just before the walk down

the aisle, so that his face will be suffused with raw emotion—
he might even cry. So it's not simply that certain events should
occur at a wedding; certain feelings and thoughts should as
well. "Tenderness, affection, and caring are the emotions you
should seek to portray in the photographs of the bride and
her mother," writes photographer George Schaub, leaving
aside how the specific mother and daughter truly feel about
one another. He has an entire chapter called "Highlighting
the Family's Closeness," as if closeness can be seen in every
family as long as you use the right flash.

Well, I suppose closeness can be seen in every family *picture*—which is all that really matters. As long as it looks right
in the pictures, it is right. Sint writes, "if my clients want to
live a fantasy day, I'll do my best to help them create one," as
if the day exists only on film and does not have its own reality. He also writes about how to "create a salable memory."
I was shocked first by the bald word *salable*, but then I realized what was wrong with the phrase was really the idea of
creating memory. The photographs are supposed to become
our memories.

And they do, at least to an extent. I don't know if I remember the house we lived in until I was three or if I'm just
remembering the photographs. Likewise, sociologist Lewis
says, the images contained in the wedding album "may tend
to mystify memories of the actual rites of the ceremony." But
I don't blame the photographers: mystification must be
what we want, or we wouldn't let them tilt our heads just so.
In fact, many photographers comment on the eagerness of a
broken family to try to appear whole again "for the record";
for the sake of posterity, the bride's dad and mom will pose
together, though they both have had new husbands for years.
And before we were married, I was more than once the subject of debate during a portrait-taking session: does the girl-
friend make it into the group photo or doesn't she? Usually

they take one with and one without, so that, if the relationship doesn't work out, my presence on that day can be erased from "memory." If the photograph were simply a historical record—who was there with whom—there would be no question of whether to include me.

So we and our photographers team up to produce these touched-up memories. Norfleet quotes photographer Bradford Bachrach: "A portrait makes us appear as everything we wish we were. It's not just a map of the face. It goes beyond a flat record. It is a person at his best—an exaltation." Lewis writes that in wedding photography, "an ideal screen is placed over real life."

One guide aimed at the bride and groom tries to address the anxiety people feel about being photographed when they know perfectly well that they are not the "ideal" bride and groom. They are afraid their pictures won't show the fantasy. But the author, Chuck DeLaney, can't quite bring himself to eschew the fantasy altogether. "Accept who you are. Take your strong features and lead with them," he says, as if that's one piece of advice, rather than two contradictory ones. He goes on to give specific advice on how to handle beauty spots, moles, excess weight, bald spots, and so on. He concludes:

> You are who you are. The person you are marrying has chosen you above all others, and loves you for who you are.
>
> Don't let the overall narrow aesthetic of beauty in our modern society make you crazy. Your wedding day is your day, and it's your day to be *yourself.*
>
> Again, you might discuss any concerns you may have with your photographer, who will be able to make suggestions about types of poses for small and large group portraits that will avoid emphasis on physical size . . .

In other words, it's your day to be yourself, but here are some ways to make that self look thinner. Because no matter how much DeLaney wishes it weren't so, people don't want to look like they look at their weddings; they want to look like they imagine themselves to look. They want to match the images in their heads, to look as shiny and perfect as all the movie stars they have seen walk down the aisle. Maybe they don't look that way in real life, but they get an extra shot on film: photographs give them a chance to create an alternate reality. That reality, captured by, created by a photograph, becomes "a reference point to which [they] can return time and again," writes Erving Goffman, "as testimonial, as evidence, as depiction, of what [their] best social [selves have] been and, by implication, must still be." Those demure photographs of my parents dressing in separate rooms did not so much reflect their real relationship as create its ideal.

The ideal representation of a relationship. It's what weddings are too. Weddings and photographs are both ways in which we self-invent, present our ideal of ourselves. The bride dances with her new father-in-law though he fought to keep her out of the family. The bride and groom make vows before a god they have until then ignored. Later they carefully dance a complete, newly acquired waltz routine, though they had never before advanced beyond the junior-high cling and grope. These actions can be read as false, as distortions of reality. And photographs of that distorted reality will be false too: the bride and groom won't end up with an accurate, historical record of who they are and how they felt. They'll end up, in the worst case, with a record of what Hollywood and their parents and their photographer's portfolio taught them a wedding was supposed to be, and who they were supposed to be.

The hardest task a couple have when they wed is holding

out against other people's images of what a wedding should be, and how a bride and groom should look and act. But if they can resist those forces, if they can build and then protect their own vision of their wedding and of themselves, they will end up with a truthful record. Maybe it won't reflect the true nature of their feelings for their in-laws, or their true comfort level on the dance floor. But the record will reflect something that may be even more important; it will reflect what at that moment they wished reality had been. When we marry we get to create a day—and a photo album—devoted to our notion of our best selves. There is truth in that, beautiful truth.

7

Civic Lesson

Filene's housewares department, mid-July. Adam and I wandered slowly past mahogany-colored cases full of Lenox, Spode, Royal Doulton, Wedgwood. Lights set into glass shelving made the china appear to gleam from within. I hunched close to Adam, as if to hide; I spoke in a hush; I was embarrassed. We were registering. Registering for china was, I thought, about as far as one could get from the idea of marriage as a profound commitment between two adults. We had arrived instead at marriage as a bonanza for greedy kids. We were calmly, matter-of-factly making a list of the things we wanted our guests to give us. It was so blatantly materialistic, so shallow, so . . . much fun. We loved things and we loved to entertain; picturing our dining room table covered with glinting crystal and china was deeply pleasing. Besides, our bridal consultant, a motherly woman in a swivel chair behind a polished desk, poised to record our choices at her keyboard, acted as if we were being quite sensible, as if making this computerized record of our greed were the natural

response of any kind-hearted bride and groom to the be-
seeching of bewildered guests. Apparently, we actually owed
it to our loved ones to spell out our desires. And she was so
solicitous, so helpful. We sat down in the thronelike upholstered chairs across from her and suddenly her desk was
transformed into our dining room table. She set a place in
front of us so we could see the various elements in combination; she knew we were not registering for silver, but here,
just for the full effect, let's try a set of Reed & Barton next to
the Villeroy & Boch. There we are.

Salespeople had been paying a great deal of attention to us
since we began making wedding plans. I wasn't used to it
and I didn't like it; the pressure underlying the pretense of
friendship made me nervous. I hadn't felt this much consumer discomfort since Adam and I had bought our car over
a year earlier. That had been long before we even thought
about picking a date to wed; looking back, though, I could
see the straight line from that moment of merchandise selection to this one. I should have known from the time we
strolled into the lot of the Honda dealership that marriage
was looming.

It wasn't because the car was our first major purchase
together, but because it was a Honda Civic. The right car for
us. The car we liberal, college-educated twenty-somethings
were demographically determined to buy. In marketing
strategy meetings, they tossed our grinning photo in the Sold
pile without a second glance.

It made me uncomfortable to own the perfect car for me.
I had become accustomed, in the five or so years I had lived
with Adam, to driving his family's cars. The Greenberg fleet
consisted of altogether inappropriate vehicles. The sportiest
was an '85 Oldsmobile sedan, dark blue, with electric locks
and windows that thumped and groaned when you used
them, as if you were asking rather a lot. Then there was an

'83 Oldsmobile station wagon, the size of two normal cars welded together, whose back seat could have doubled as a guest bedroom. I should not have been driving either of those cars: I was not old enough or patriotic enough or heedless enough of global warming or a good enough parallel parker. And I took great pleasure in driving them anyway. But my favorite vehicle to clamber out of was the Ford three-quarter-ton pickup. I have never thought of myself as slight—especially at college, where I first drove the truck, and where the thickest thing about my female classmates was their winter-weight Lycra—but in the Ford I felt like a mere slip of a thing. This truck was built to accommodate a three-hundred-pound construction worker. This was a bacon-double-cheeseburger truck, and I was a confirmed salad eater. I loved it.

The little green Honda we decided to buy, on the other hand, was definitely vegetable matter. That car and I were meant for each other. When I drove it, I would no longer be a diamond in the rough of a gas-guzzler; I would be a diamond in the shiny new ring of a well-made, fuel-efficient import. No one at the health-food co-op, the public radio station, or the art-house cinema would be surprised to see me drive up: it was precisely the car they would expect. And I like to defy expectation, not satisfy it; my thinking was that the world, especially the corporate world, was too full already of satisfied expectation. I hate to be one of the multitudes lining up at the cineplex on opening day to see an overhyped summer flick designed to appeal to my sex and age group, mechanically handing over eight dollars to enrich both a global media corporation and a monopoly cinema chain. Just as they had banked on. I wanted to be unpredictable, indefinable, uncategorizable.

On the other hand, I was irked that the Honda salesman basically ignored me; he insisted on acting as if Adam alone were making this decision. Adam introduced me as "My girl-friend, Kate" and the salesman clearly couldn't figure out whether I was the kind of girlfriend who'd accompanied Adam to three overhyped summer flicks or the kind of girl-friend who'd accompanied him to seven family weddings and a funeral. Until then I would have been amused by his confusion; I would have enjoyed wearing the disguise of that hard-shifting, poor-handling word, *girlfriend*. I would have loved the fact that he couldn't properly categorize me. But now it frustrated me. Didn't he know how important I was? Couldn't he tell I was Adam's life's partner, his better half, his . . .

It was then that I yearned for the word *wife*.

A wedding is essentially all of society's expectations tied up in a weekend package. And planning a wedding, in a time and a place where most marrying couples are relatively free to do as they please, is largely a matter of deciding how many of those expectations you want to defy and how many you want to fulfill. I realized, when we started to get down to the details that summer, that Adam and I wanted to ful-fill a shocking number. I didn't even consider not wearing white. It took about two minutes for us, confirmed nonbe-lievers, to decide to have a Jewish wedding. Wedding party? You mean divide our friends into some sort of hierarchy, hurt some people's feelings, and force others to rent tuxes? Why not?

And there we were at Filene's, choosing between Lenox's Hannah Platinum and Federal Platinum as if informing our guests that we would welcome the donation of eighty-dollar place settings (should we ask for twelve or sixteen?) were the most natural thing in the world. As if we didn't already eat our dinners on perfectly acceptable plates.

When you enter the wedding world, you discover it to be full of the strangest customs, customs that all the other inhabitants of that world treat as normal. A random glance at a *Bride's* magazine reveals advice on such surreal matters as how to be gracious in a receiving line, how to maneuver in a dress that requires several times your normal clearance space, how to cut a tiered cake into even slices, how to toss a bouquet fairly. The assumption, of course, is that all of these bizarre rituals will be part of your wedding. And the assumption creeps into you, too—or crept, many years ago, when you weren't watching.

I don't remember playing "wedding" as a girl, but anecdotal evidence shows me to have been unusual in this. I didn't play with Barbie dolls, either; my parents steered us more toward stuffed animals, books, board games, and Erector sets. Children who do play with Barbie dolls get a lot of exposure to the wedding fantasy and all of its strange trappings: eToys lists twenty-nine toys under the subject of "wedding," nine of which are Barbie-related. You can get an ivory Barbie wedding dress, or a white one trimmed in pink, silver, or fur; you can get Barbie Wedding Fantasy Bride Shoes and an entire Barbie Bridal Boutique, which, according to the eToys description, is "the perfect place to take care of all the wedding necessities." Those necessities include a tiara, earrings, purse, shoes, gown, and veil. All the toys listed contribute to our culture-wide concept of what is "necessary" at a wedding: Cinderella's Wedding, a Madame Alexander doll, includes a white satin, full-skirted gown trimmed in lace and a net veil; Flower Girl and Ring Bearer dolls by Effanbee imply, of course, that flower girls and ring bearers are essential to matrimony, as are rings on lace-trimmed pillows, and baskets of flowers; Wedding Playscene by Learning Curve includes felt cutouts of bride, groom, bridesmaid, bouquet, and wedding present; Wedding Fantasy Party, a Barbie Entertaining Set, sports a decorated wedding cake with a cake topper, champagne glasses, and a "diamond" ring.

All of these toys naturally enough emphasize the playthings (costume, gifts, wedding cake) and the games (tossing the bouquet, marching down the aisle, scattering the flowers) custom has associated with American weddings. As do movies, books, and television, all of which seem to reside in the back of the mind ready to emerge unquestioned at the prospect of matrimony. So when it's time to plan your own wedding, even if you're an independent-minded person, you wind up considering some very odd things, considering, as sociologist Beatrice Gottlieb puts it, "an extraordinary amount of ritualistic behavior that is only dimly understood but nevertheless eagerly engaged in." When my older sister was planning her wedding a few years before mine, she called me to discuss whether they should "do the garter thing." That's when the groom, encircled by the wedding guests, and preferably under spotlight, pulls a garter off the bride and tosses it to the assembled males, the lucky one of whom then gets to place it on the leg of the woman who caught the bouquet. Amy said, "Do you think we should do the garter thing?" I said, "What?" (Disbelief.) She said, "Well, I'm going to be throwing a bouquet and I thought it would only be fair if Chris got to throw something." This woman was marrying a younger man of an entirely different religious and cultural background; she was no slave to tradition. I said, "What?" (Indignation.) Didn't she realize that the implication behind these rituals was that single women were clamoring for marriage (in the form of a bouquet), whereas single men were clamoring for sex (in the form of a garter)? And that is exactly the sort of sensible, analytical thing a person might say before entering the wedding world, where some other brain seems to take over. Where tradition rules almost unchallenged. Eighty percent of American brides have their garters tossed. (My sister, incidentally, did not end up in their ranks, though she did toss a bouquet.) It's not surprising that 80 percent of American women wouldn't read a sexist meaning into this tradition. But consider how many of them, since most women today wear pantyhose rather than stockings held up by garters, actually had to go out and purchase an outdated piece of underwear in order to have their grooms throw it. Tradition is stronger than common sense, and it is stronger than politics. Even in the radical seventies, according to Marcia Seligson, "at a time when love-ins, live-ins, and hippie weddings were throwing brickbats at tradition, 94 percent of American brides still chose to be married in white." As Barbara Norfleet commented drily, "nudists still wear veils."

I realize that a lot of these customs have origins that pre-date the wedding industry. Dressing all your friends alike, for instance, is not just a department store conspiracy; it comes from ancient superstition. "In the days when evil spirits were thought to be a potential threat to any ceremony," writes Tad Tuleja in *Curious Customs*, "a married couple dressed its friends in costumes identical or similar to their own, to confuse the demons." Fine. Good plan. But I had no real worries about demons other than ones to whom I was directly related, and they could probably pick me out in a crowd. No need for that precaution, then, right?

And yet it takes a startling amount of resolution to decide *not* to do needless things, just because those things have worked their way into matrimonial tradition. Things you wouldn't even consider in real life—like putting four differently shaped women all in matching dresses that suit the one woman of the group who isn't wearing it. For years, I had questioned this practice in the wake of other people's color-coded weddings, or in commiseration with some woeful, full-hipped future bridesmaid holding an expensive purple drop-waisted dress. No, no, I couldn't possibly do that to women I loved. Could I? Somewhere in my brain played a slideshow of wedding photos, the way they were *supposed* to look. I guess they could all wear the same color, I thought, or I could buy them all a certain fabric and . . . Then I had a brilliant idea: black bottoms (which everyone has) and white tops (which everyone can afford and use later), will look good with tuxes—perfect. But one of my prospective dress-up dolls complained that she didn't look good in two-piece outfits; another really wanted to wear *color*. The word "waitress" was mentioned, and "sterile," and then I came to. Forget it, I said: everyone wears what she wants. And that was the tortuous process by which I returned to what, in the nonbridal world, could be described only as sanity.

At work somewhere deep within me—as well as, of course, all around me—was a potent combination of social expectation and commerce. *That* must be one of the happiest marriages on record. It is certainly one of the wealthiest: American weddings support a more than 50-billion-dollar industry. This figure encompasses not only the celebrations themselves, the average cost of which is $20,000, but also the gifts, the loot for which we were so conscientiously register-ing. We weren't as conscientious as we might have been, though. According to the bridal registry checklists you can find in every wedding magazine, to be a truly appropriate pair of newlyweds, we would need six kinds of spoons, four kinds of forks, five kinds of knives. We would need glasses for red wine, white wine, champagne, iced beverages, cocktails, highballs, old-fashioneds, beer, brandy, sherry, liqueur, Irish coffee, and fruit juice. Our new home would be incomplete without shower massage, electric toothbrush, fax machine, cappuccino maker, juicer, and exercise equipment. "I'm think-ing of not registering for china," writes one beleaguered bride to the *Bride's* magazine "Home Q&A." "Everyone tells me I'm crazy. But where would I store all those dishes in my small home?" The correct answer is, "Don't worry, all you need is something to eat on and enough money left over for something to eat." But that wasn't what *Bride's* said, perhaps because the expert the magazine consulted was a representative of Royal Worcester and Spode.

One has to tread so carefully to avoid buying twenty-five centerpieces, or party favors everyone will throw away, or new underwear no one will see except one exhausted man. I fought the bridal industry, I succumbed to it, but only once did I feel I was becoming a wedding cliché. A Bride. Bridal magazines are, for one, called "bridal" magazines, as is the "bridal" registry, where a "bridal" consultant will help you; the assumption of the marital-commercial complex is that the woman is the one who plans the weddings, covets the sherry glasses, and will spend an exorbitant amount on a dress. There are occasional articles on grooms who plan weddings—"He Did It His Way: A Groom Plans the Wedding and Lives to Tell About It"—but they treat the whole idea as a humorous anomaly, to be tolerated only in extreme circumstances, such as, say, a bridal coma. While pretending to believe it's possible for a man to plan a wedding, such articles (and even the occasional slim volume) perpetuate the stereotype of the feckless groom; they crack jokes about twenty-four beer mugs on the registry and no vegetables at the reception. Most articles forget the groom altogether, or give him as much column space as the caterer or dressmaker: a sample to-do list might include the fiancé in seven of forty-three bridal chores. Six Months Before, item 3: Meet with fiancé to discuss rehearsal dinner.

Our wedding was a project Adam and I did together; I did not have to schedule meetings with him. So even when I felt overtaken by the wedding industry, as among the shining

silver displays at Filene's, I still felt a bit of a resister. It was
the bridal registry, true, but Adam and I were there together,
equally involved in the process of outfitting our home. In fact,
he chose our china pattern. But once, as I said, I felt like the
typical bride. Right when I got back from Italy, we had to put
together our wedding invitations. It started out well enough:
We came up with the wording while planting pumpkins on
an early summer evening; Adam chopped a little dent in the
soil with his hoe, I dropped in four or five seeds, and he pat-
ted the soil back over them, over and over, up and down the
rows. To this rhythm, as the sun was setting, we decided
that our parents should be the inviters (that tradition passed
scrutiny since they were the hosts of the wedding) but that
we wouldn't use "Dr. and Mrs." The invitation had a solemn
ring, but the words were ours—no "request the honor of your
presence" or "reception immediately following." So far, we
thought, so un-stereotypical.

But we were stumped about how the invitations should
look. After trying and failing to think of any classy, cheap,
and inventive way to design them, we ended up on the living
room floor with a thick book of traditional wedding invitation styles, about ten of which were satisfactory. And that
was as far as Adam could go. He moved to a sofa and turned
his attention fully to the Orioles game; I was left in hyper-
bridal mode, chattering questions at his profile about fonts
and finishes and papers until he couldn't stand it anymore:
"I don't care! Just pick something," he said, managing still to
keep his eyes on the television. I felt sick, not because he'd
snapped at me, not because I couldn't decide, but because
we had skidded alarmingly into cliché: groom watches sports,
bride pesters. Social expectation completely fulfilled.

Along the wedding way, but for that small loss of control, we managed mostly—after struggling far more than we
would have expected—to steer clear of traditions in which

we found no meaning. Meaning is what gets lost, we thought, when you automatically do things the way everybody else does. That's why clichés, even well-chosen clichés, are bad writing: they keep a reader's brain from working. Throw a bouquet and nobody thinks about what that might mean; throw an orange, and everybody does. Well, I didn't carry a bouquet and I wasn't given away and there was no tiered cake with plastic figures on top. Veils and garters had too many sexist connotations for me, and I couldn't figure out why I would want to be encumbered by high heels and a train, since I am perfectly capable of tripping barefoot over the hem of my bathrobe. To my mother's gentle disappointment I shrugged off the borrowed/blue/old/new thing, and Adam and I slept together in my parents' home throughout the prewedding week—no pretend first meeting at the altar. An hour before we walked down the aisle, he had, as planned, buttoned me into my white dress.

Unfortunately for someone who wants to marry untraditionally, altering the traditional wedding ceremony is itself a hallowed wedding tradition, at least in America. We're supposed to be individuals, right? So we get married on a boat or we plant a tree after the ceremony or we have an aria sung during it. Bridal magazines are full of ideas on how to be "different": "50 Ways to Leave Your Reception," "A New Direction in Attendants' Dresses." You can be sure that those hippie brides wearing white in the seventies were also, defiantly, walking up the aisle barefoot or braless or to the tune of "Blowin' in the Wind."

All of our little distinctions, all of our carefully thought-out decisions were, finally, a kind of vanity. They were the rough equivalent of the thin coating of farm dust that covered our new Honda. They didn't fool anyone. We were getting married. For years we had resisted, for years we had lived together, defying social expectation in a small way at least by acting married while not being married. But now we were doing it, we were getting married. And no matter how you do it or when, getting married is a deeply conventional thing to do. A convention is a meeting, a coming together; in the sense of tradition, it is a coming together of social expectations, a cultural agreement. When you marry, you sign the agreement. In a way, since wedding wouldn't change anything practical in our very domestic, very married lives, the *only* thing that Adam and I were doing was accepting the convention. If our wedding was indeed a means of self-expression, a statement of our beliefs and personality, we had hoped to say how different we were, how unique: uniquely connected already, uniquely stable as a couple, uniquely thoughtful. But what we were really saying, simply by marrying, was, We're the same. Yes, in fact, we do belong. We will sign that cultural agreement. We will take part in an institution that excludes some, oppresses others, and fails at least a third. An institution that is exalted by politicians we abhor and promoted by an industry as spiritually meaningful as a mall on Christmas Eve.

Marrying in and of itself was conventional; marrying *each other* was about as conventional as could be. Nothing about us as a couple was surprising: we were both white, both Jewish, both well educated; he was a few years older than I. We were that perfect balance of endogamy and exogamy: we shared ethnic and socioeducational status, but no blood. Our parents were all professionals: my mother was a college administrator and his was a special education teacher; my father was an English professor and his was an ear, nose, and throat doctor. Our fathers had always treated each other gingerly, unsure perhaps of the other's world, or insecure in it, but respectful of it. "The ideal case was prestige marrying wealth," writes Beatrice Gottlieb, in her history of the Western family. "Among Jews a rabbi's son or daughter lent prestige to a merchant's family, whose wealth was welcomed in turn by the rabbi." That summer, as we inched toward inter-relating, I started to think of our fathers as two shtetl Jews who'd made a good match between their children. Marrying in the faith—now *that's* conventional. A distant cousin told me warmly a few years before that I was a "good girl" for dating a Jew; she had just learned that my sister Amy was marrying a Lutheran and my sister Sady was dating an Epis-copalian. And instantly I didn't want to be good if that's how people defined good, I didn't want to fulfill expectations born of prejudice. I wanted to challenge stereotypes, to make peo-ple look twice. Think twice. To me, Amy was the good girl, for marrying out: the son of a minister, and a westerner, to boot. That was risky, that was brave, that was making a human connection beyond the predictable bounds. My high-school boyfriend, Matt, an Irish Catholic, had recently married a Zulu. As a rule, our society doesn't imagine dark skin next to light skin in the wedding photos; less than two percent of all married couples in America are racially intermarried. Matt, when he wed, showed society's imagination to be limited; in doing so maybe he even pushed those limits a little farther out. Forgoing the bouquet tradition doesn't really compare.

One night after dinner at Adam's parents' house, as I lis-tened to Adam's father discuss the wedding on the phone with my father, I had a sudden image of them, belly to belly on a village street, gesturing jovially in *Fiddler on the Roof* costumes. I was clearing the table, helping Adam's mom put away the leftovers and put out the brownies I had baked. And I realized that it wasn't just my Jewishness that made me a good catch in the world of the shtetl; I, the daughter-in-law-to-be, fit this scene in every way: polite to my elders, good-natured, a good cook who abhorred waste and spent hot kitchen hours canning summer produce—and those large hips would be perfect for bearing children. I was the car Adam was demographically determined to drive. And he, hard-working, reliable, good with kids, was my Honda Civic.

That day in Filene's, and increasingly all summer, I had to accept that I was or was turning into the person my culture expected me to be. I always thought I was different from the mainstream, independent, an outsider looking in. But weddings have a way of making you realize how much of your culture you have absorbed, how little, finally, you are willing to reject. Or are capable of rejecting. When you find yourself planning to stand up in a white dress, repeating the same words your mother and her mother repeated, it hits you, hard, just how much like everyone else you really are.

Maybe that's not simply an unfortunate consequence of the process of marrying; maybe that's actually part of what we seek when we marry. In *The Art of Loving*, psychoanalyst Eric Fromm argues that "the deepest need of man . . . is the need to overcome his separateness, to leave the prison of his aloneness." Intimate connection with a lover is one way to fulfill the "longing for union"; but to have that connection, you don't have to get married. Adam and I did not plan to marry in order to make a connection between us—that was already there, had been there for years. Fromm points out, though, that another way to fill the "need for love and union" is through community. He puts it rather starkly:

In contemporary Western society the union with the group is the prevalent way of overcoming separateness. . . . If I am like everybody else, if I have no feelings or thoughts which make me different, if I conform in custom, dress, ideas, to the pattern of the group, I am saved; saved from the frightening experience of aloneness.

In marrying each other, Adam and I married, in a sense, our community. To the extent that we conformed, to the extent that we went through and experienced what most other Americans experience at some point in their lives, we removed that sense of separation between ourselves and everyone else.

According to the 1990 census, Americans marry in great numbers. Only 9 percent of Americans had still never married by the time they turned 44. Marriage rates in the United States are among the world's highest. Perhaps the explanation for that lies in the essential aloneness of modern Americans. Ours today is a heterogenous culture, a country in which our neighbors probably do not share our religion, ethnicity, educational background, politics, taste. A country of transients, of strangers, in which the people next door are likely to have moved in only recently, and to limit their contact to a brief wave, a nod of the head. We just don't have that much in common with one another.

But there is one thing. Marriage is still an almost universal goal, and the wedding is still almost universally accepted as its crystallized moment of happiness, the moment to which we all look forward eagerly or look back wistfully. Ninety percent of Americans may marry, but a whopping ninety-six percent say they want to. Is there another event in our lives that we all yearn for? Most Americans, of all races, religions, and ethnicities, have children, but the *event* involved in that—giving birth—is not the focus of universal fantasy. Only women actually go through it, and most of them dread it. And children certainly don't play at it: eToys, though it has anatomically correct premie dolls and race-specific infant dolls that can wet their pants, has no Delivery Room Playscene, or, for that matter, anything for children under the topic "labor" or "childbirth." Children don't play at it and they don't fantasize about it. But childhood is precisely when weddings first enter our imaginations. From that point, we imagine weddings ever after, seeking out those images in movies and books, reading of celebrity weddings in *People* and noncelebrity weddings in the local daily, tuning in when TV shows have their characters marry during sweeps week. How can the networks be sure we will watch? Because the only universal rite of passage in America is the wedding. It's the only reliable way we have to reach across the barriers between us, to connect.

"Most people are not even aware of their need to conform," says Fromm. "They live under the illusion that they follow their own ideas and inclinations, that they are individualists, that they have arrived at their opinions as the result of their own thinking—and that it just happens that their ideas are the same as those of the majority." Adam and I were not this oblivious—we didn't really believe we'd invented the idea of the wedding party or the first dance. But certainly our impulses toward social customs took us by surprise. As did the sense of community that marrying gave us. Fromm describes the connection that people make with the group (or with one another in a sexual relationship) as a relief of tension, a respite from the anxiety of aloneness. And something really did relax that summer, some barrier in us, or between us and the world.

At first I resisted it, as I resisted my wedding shower, which I thought of as the apex of conformity. My mother-in-law wanted to throw me one, which discomfitted me, but also pleased me. Part of me revolted against the idea of a celebration that excluded men; Adam and I were proud of both having male and female friends, of not being a boys'-night-out, girls'-night-out kind of couple. But I like attention and I like presents, and part of me wanted a party just for me. All the women on the street and in the near neighborhood came, a couple of whom I had met only once or twice. These women are neighbors, good neighbors, but in the modern American sense. They don't gather together to sew or can or make soap or stir vats of apple butter; they don't watch each other's children. They wave to each other from their Volvos. There had never been such a gathering at my mother-in-law's before, in other words, and there may well not be again. But that shower felt good, it felt like a warm memory of some vanished time, when neighbors were neighbors for life and women regularly passed on to one another their wisdom and their recipes. Across generations, across religion, across class, across the political spectrum, these women joked and advised and connected with one another in memory or in anticipation of this shared experience: the wedding.

At Filene's I wandered over to inspect the coffee pots, and I saw a man making notes on a registry form. I said, "Got some decisions to make, don't you?" and he grinned, "I guess so." And I said, "All by yourself? That's not fair." He shrugged and said, "Well, that's the way she wants it." It felt good to talk to a stranger like that, with no introduction and no ice-breaking, to feel as if you understand one another right away, to connect even briefly. The way you feel waiting out a lightning storm in a restaurant, when you start talking to the people around you, as if everyone were part of the same party. As if you weren't alone. The way you feel, even, in a mall on Christmas Eve. Everything seems to loosen—the anxiety of separateness is relieved momentarily—and you say to the person standing in line ahead of you, "Oh, how lovely—where did you get that?" Or "Boy, you must have bought out the scarf department." Maybe that crazy dash through the mall isn't spiritually meaningless, after all; it may have little to do with the birth of Jesus, but it seems to have much to do with human connection, with union. Why else, with all the stress and expense of the holiday, can it still leave you feeling full and satisfied?

Christmas Eve is one of those moments of community that somehow survive spiritually despite commercialization. Like weddings. I don't believe marrying changed the love between me and Adam, sanctified it or even solidified it. But I know it changed our relationship to the world. Adam and I had never felt as charged with love as we did the summer we planned our wedding, love for strangers in malls, for brides and grooms, for husbands and wives, for all people who make their way through life. In that way, conforming to society, marrying at last, as shocking as it was to my sense of myself as an individual, *was* a relief. And so would be the word I had longed for, the word that would now fit, the word *wife*.

~ 8 ~

Gathering Home

The Orioles were playing the Rangers. Camden Yards glowed bright, the players in white against the green grass, framed by the red brick of the warehouse and the blue of the sky. Late July at the ballpark. Adam and I were in Baltimore on our way home from a week of prewedding chores in Virginia, a month before the wedding. We try to go to a game at least once a year; Adam loves the O's and I love the park— the smells and the sounds and the people but mostly the dazzle of the diamond and its Baltimore backdrop. It makes me feel like I'm part of something, like I'm an American, like being an American is a good thing. That summer, as a bride, about to take part in the only common American rite of passage, I felt even more connected to the crowd around me, even more a part of the scene. There we sat, an American couple in the heat of a summer afternoon: Adam, in his black and orange cap, with his hot dog and his Coke; next to him, me, his fiancée, leaning over to ask him why the hitter was bunting. Next to me, Gerald Serotta, our rabbi.

Rabbi Serotta was "ours" in only the most limited sense. He was not the rabbi either of us grew up with, the rabbi who married our parents, the rabbi who officiated at Adam's bar or my bat mitzvah ceremonies, or the rabbi who lived next door. He was simply the rabbi who would marry us. He was a good friend of a friend, and the rabbi of the George Washington University Hillel, and we had sought him out in April and asked him, shyly, to marry us. That day in late July we had spoken with him at his home about the ceremony. The ballgame we drove to afterward was supposed to be a way to get to know each other before the wedding.

It was an awkward courtship. We were conscious that every word we spoke would constitute a large percentage of what our rabbi knew about us. We wanted him to have some sense of the couple he was marrying, so we gestured and speed-talked and interrupted each other to try to tell him who we were—along with what kind of ceremony we imagined and when he had to show up where. And we wanted to like him, too, wanted to feel that a good person would be marrying us, a person who could be our friend, even if he wasn't. An hour at his house and nine innings at the ballpark would be precious little time.

We wanted, for the few minutes of our wedding ceremony, to feel as if our officiant really were "our rabbi," to have the sort of trust and warmth and history with him connoted by those words. But it was absurd to expect such a connection to materialize from the thin air of our completely secular lives. Adam and I had no rabbi. We belonged to no synagogue, and we never attended one, except to celebrate other peoples' rites of passage. Neither of us would think of consulting a rabbi for advice. Neither of us believed in God. And yet we wanted a man in a *tallis* (a prayer shawl) with a gray beard and wise eyes to bless our matrimony. We wanted a Jewish wedding.

There hadn't been many chores left to take care of in Virginia that week, the week that ended at the O's game with the rabbi. Dress and tuxedo fittings, consultations with the rental place and the florist. Other than that, it was more a time to think through the wedding weekend, to rehearse it in our heads. One morning we went to the site where the ceremony would take place, a modern lecture hall in the education building/dairy barn of the Museum of American Frontier Culture. We had to decide how the room should be configured, how many chairs should be set out and in what way. My father, who has a good spatial imagination and a trained theater sense, sketched our options for us. We imagined and reimagined our friends and family in that space, until we managed to squeeze everyone in, until they could all see and hear. We kept imagining them as we walked back to the outside of the building to decide how they would enter and exit; we pictured dresses and suits against the rural backdrop, heard high heels crunch in the gravel.

Summoned forth in my head, our guests continued to hover as we went to lunch at the Little Grill. The Grill was a hangout during my high school years; it's small and scruffy, with a few booths and a few freestanding tables with mismatched wooden chairs. My friends and I would meet there after school for shareable food—nachos and french fries—and the Grill's laid-back staff would let us take up a table for hours. Or I would sit there alone killing time before my mother got off work; I would sip Red Zinger tea from a chipped mug and read, or let my eyes wander over posted notices for poetry readings long since quiet, used guitars long since sold. I wasn't alone, really, since I knew most of the customers and all of the waiters ("waiters" makes them sound too formal; picture a friend with his hand on your chair, offering to bring you something to eat). Now when I ate there on trips home, I knew one or two people by name, and a few more looked familiar. But my long absence and the constant flux of a college town meant that mostly I didn't know them, and not knowing the people in a place that felt so much like home always made me lonely.

When we came to lunch there during our week of chores, I filled the Grill with people I knew, people I loved; I brought all our invited guests along in my head. I pictured every chair occupied by a loved one—there were my first cousins over at the counter joking with the cook; there was our wedding party taking up the big round table in the middle. The Grill is a small space, and a lot of people had to stand as they sipped their iced teas and cream sodas, but that was OK because, in my imagination, they wanted to get to know one another anyway. I watched them move from table to table, heard the loud and happy hum of their conversation. I looked forward to our wedding.

The first Jewish wedding I went to (at age seventeen) was of my aunt Leslie to Dave, who, though raised in a Protestant home, does not believe in any religion. They had lived in Cambridge, Massachusetts, for years, but they married at Leslie's father's lakehouse an hour from Montgomery, her home town. Their *huppah* (wedding canopy) was the gazebo Granddaddy had specially built on the swimming deck. Their rabbi was from Granddaddy's synagogue; he had known Leslie as a teenager, but he hadn't seen her since. Until, that is, they met to discuss the wedding.

Six years later, Adam's brother Josh married Kate, who was Jewish by birth and sense of identity, but had attended synagogue, by her count, only two or three times growing up. They lived in Somerville, Massachusetts, didn't belong to a congregation, but observed the major holidays with one or the other's family. They married at Kate's family's cabin in

Maine, under a huppah made from quilt squares they had asked loved ones to contribute. I carefully signed the *ketubah* (marriage contract) as a witness, copying the Hebrew letters of my name that the rabbi had written out. Actually, he was a cantor, whom Josh and Kate had brought up from Boston. He humorously explained the Jewish ceremony to the guests, and he spoke at length about Josh and Kate and their ethical concerns. He knew about Josh and Kate and their ethical concerns because they had met with him before the wedding to tell him.

My sister Amy married Chris the next year. From San Francisco they searched for a rabbi in the Virginia area who would marry them, a Jew and the son of a Lutheran minister. After many rejections and not a few insults, they finally found a likely rabbi in D.C. He denounced Lutheranism throughout their meeting, but he agreed to marry them, for a hefty fee. They felt they had no option but to hire him. They married at an inn not far from my parents' house; their huppah was a square of lined silk into which a friend had cross-stitched their portraits. They worried that the rabbi would carelessly present them to the guests after the ceremony as "Mr. and Mrs. Chris Gopp," even though Chris was changing his name to Cohen. That's how little "their rabbi" knew them.

Of these six brides and grooms—eight including us—only my sister attends synagogue on anything like a regular basis (and less now than she did before she married, partly because Jewish officialdom had treated Chris so poorly). Yet we all went to considerable trouble to have Jewish weddings, to have the huppah and ketubah and the rabbi, to say the few Hebrew words necessary to make the ceremony officially Jewish.

The phenomenon of unaffiliated people having religious weddings is not, apparently, unusual. Many more people have religious weddings than are religious, even if you count as "religious" merely spotty church or synagogue attendance. WeddingBells.com, a wedding planning website, notes, "A lot of brides and grooms these days are up against the problem of wanting a religious ceremony, but without having set foot in a place of worship in a long, long time." Among *Modern Bride* magazine readers, 87 percent of first-time brides have a religious ceremony. But only 38 percent of U.S. adults say they attend church or synagogue weekly—and sociologists, using attendance counts, suggest that that self-reported statistic is actually double the real number. "Young people are opting for church marriages in numbers that exhaust the clergy," announces a recent news article, adding, "they are not necessarily returning to the church itself." Wedding planning books have sections on how to find a clergyman; a wedding website, blissezine.com, suggests, "If you're the bride and groom, you'll want to be familiar with the basic customs of your religion." Clearly, even a faintly observant bride or groom would already have a clergyman, would already be familiar with his or her religion. Such advice, along with websites like Rent-a-Priest.com and services like Wedding Bells Clergy, is aimed at the great number of marrying people who want a religious ceremony, but not a religious life.

An early section of Anita Diamant's *The New Jewish Wedding* is entitled "Choosing a Rabbi"; it gives tips on how to find one and how to tell if he or she is right for you. "If you wouldn't pick a dentist at random, don't try that approach with a rabbi," Diamant advises. These words of wisdom are unimaginable in an Old World scenario, in which the bride and groom would have grown up in the same community, with the same rabbi. There would have been no need to meet with the rabbi to make sure he knew what kind of people he was marrying, no need to fly him to the wedding site, no need for him to explain the ceremony to the guests as he conducted it. In that kind of close-knit Jewish community, as Diamant points out, "No one needed a book such as this one." The bride and groom wouldn't have *chosen* a rabbi any more than they would have *chosen* to have a Jewish wedding.

Adam and I were both raised in consciously Jewish homes. Adam's was more or less Conservative: his mother, who had converted to Judaism to marry his father (and now has little patience for organized religion), keeps a kosher kitchen; his father attends an Orthodox shul. But it was rebellious too: when ordered by their father to wear their *kippot* (skull-caps), Adam and his brothers sometimes wore their Orioles caps instead, arguing that, technically, they had only to keep their heads covered—God didn't say with what. My upbringing was beyond Reform—sausage and biscuits by the Christmas tree—but strongly Jewish-identified—*shabbos* (sabbath) dinner every Friday night without fail. Both of us call ourselves Jewish, and not just out of loyalty to the underdog faith; we feel Jewish. And we enjoy the festivity and the food of the holidays, and we value the life lessons some of those holidays teach.

But we both have doubts about the basic decency of organized religion, and doubts about the specific decency of our own. We are bothered by the pettiness and the prejudice that often attach to what is meant to be religious observance. And we do not, as I said, believe in a Supreme Being—the Jewish one or anyone else's. We get a stronger sense of spirituality, of universal love and power from our favorite novels and poems than from the Torah. And it gives my soul greater uplift to walk from the tunnel into the light at Camden Yards than to enter the sanctuary of any synagogue I have yet attended.

We were not, in other words, merely unaffiliated Jews, lapsed from laziness or lack of interest, using our wedding as a point of return to the faith. We did not intend for our married home to be any more Jewish than our unmarried home. So why a Jewish wedding? We, who were trying to do everything so thoughtfully, so carefully, why would we choose to marry under the aegis of a religion we didn't believe in? We, who could no longer attend synagogue services even on Yom Kippur (the holiest day of the Jewish year) because it felt so false to read aloud words we didn't mean, why were we willing to say, "By this ring you are consecrated to me in accordance with the traditions of Moses and Israel"? What did we care about the traditions of Moses and Israel? Why do nonbelievers still believe in religious weddings?

I was bat mitzvah at age thirteen. Even at thirteen I didn't believe in God; I believed in family and in learning, I believed in my ability to conduct a service by myself, chant in Hebrew, and give a better exegesis on my Torah portion than the rabbi could. This was not, in short, a religious experience. My Hebrew knowledge was of the phonetic variety: I could read the sounds that the letters made, but I couldn't have translated more than twenty words. I said the *sh'ma*, the *aleinu*, and the mourner's *kaddish* with pleasure in the feel of them on my tongue, but without understanding.

The first time I said the kaddish as a mourner was when my grandfather died. I was eighteen. My father was wrecked after the funeral—we were all wrecked, and wrung out and wandering about the house in Montgomery trying to comprehend that Granddaddy was gone. All of a sudden, the quiet broke: relatives and congregants and the rabbi flooded through the front door into the living room and opened their prayer books and started to say the kaddish. Automatically we straightened ourselves, stood in the loose semicircle they had formed, and joined in. Someone handed us each a small, dark, cloth-covered book. The rabbi said, "Turn to page 154," and we did. In fact, the whole week, the rabbi, the congregants, and the prayer book told us what to do. We didn't have to figure out when to bury Granddaddy or where or in what kind of coffin; we didn't have to figure out when to gather to celebrate him and what to say when we did. The few people who wanted to say something not in the script had an appointed moment at which to do so. All of the rules, all of the rituals were written down in that book, and there was even a man with a gray beard who'd studied the book long and hard, who had led mourners through many other funerals, to tell us what page to turn to and how many people had to hoist the coffin. We had to decide who those people would be, but there were guidelines about that, too. "Weddings and funerals," my father said then. "That's what religion is good for. Weddings and funerals."

Did Adam and I simply need some long-established structure to follow? Did we simply want to be told exactly what to do? Is that why we had a Jewish wedding? Is that why people have religious weddings? In a memoir recounting her return to Judaism from a fully assimilated, secular life, Anne Roiphe writes:

> If one leaves the tight world of one's ancestors, if one abandons the synagogue . . . what replacements are made in the building of the soul? How are the crises of life marked: birth, marriage, death? . . . Men and women need ways of living within ethical frameworks, ways of passing on to their children their morality and their lifestyles . . . what do we in our empty apartments do to make furniture and fabric for ourselves?

When I read these words, at a table that Adam built, by the light that flows through curtains we sewed together, I am not entirely sympathetic to Roiphe's metaphor, or to her lament. Can't one provide an ethical framework for one's children without organized religion? Can't one mark the crises of life outside of a church or synagogue? It would be harder, of course, but I believe (as I must, since I am a nonbeliever) that it is possible. And that framework and those ceremonies that one creates—the furniture that one builds oneself—may be more personally meaningful than those one inherits, since they are constructed to suit one's true needs.

Adam and I thought about writing our entire ceremony from scratch. We thought about asking a friend to marry us, a local mayor, a good, thoughtful man, not Jewish. But making a ceremony from scratch would be like having someone say to us, Here's a big blank canvas. Paint a picture of your love for each other, including how it relates to your love for your family and your place in the community, and what you promise one another. Daunted, we chose instead to color in someone else's black-and-white sketch, even though we planned to draw outside the lines and use pink for the sky instead of blue. We have two beloved friends who are determined to have a wedding that is an honest and true expression of themselves and their love, not one that simply mimics other people's weddings. They know that creating this wedding, this completely original ceremony, might take years; to take the pressure off, they are considering the possibility of having children first.

These friends say they don't want to have the kind of wedding most people have, the kind constructed for the guests or the family rather than for the bride and groom. They won't, if they create their ceremony from scratch. But Adam and I started from an ancient pattern not just because creating our own would have been too difficult, not just because *we* needed the structure, but because we felt that our guests might too. A new language of ceremony, based on a wholly personal vocabulary, may be the most honest form in which to communicate one's love to one's future spouse, but it speaks to a community of only two. We can do that at home. To communicate our love and life to our friends and family, we chose a language we have in common with them.

By using the common language of a Jewish wedding, we

said that marrying wasn't just about us, it was about them too; it was about our parents and our parents' weddings, about our grandparents, about our cousins. Our wedding may not have been exactly like theirs, but it was still a wedding they could understand, it was still a wedding that might remind them of theirs—if only for the duration of nine words of Hebrew, if only for the presence of a man in a tallis with a gray beard and wise eyes.

True, our friends and family aren't all, or even mostly, Jewish. But it was a religious wedding. And everyone recognizes the officiant who stands awaiting the bride and groom, everyone recognizes the chairs fanning back in rows, and the aisle between them, everyone expects the bride and groom to wear special clothes, to stand near one another, to exchange rings, to pledge something to each other, to receive blessings, to kiss. Everyone understands and expects, on some level, a religious wedding.

We do too, I suppose. Finally it may be true that even if we thought we were starting from scratch, we would in fact be starting from learned vocabulary, from dimly remembered sounds, from internalized notions of a wedding. The furniture Adam makes, though he does not use written plans, is based on all the furniture he has seen and used in his life; it is patterned on received ideas of Bed and Desk and Table. So any ceremony we thought we had invented would probably mimic (or comment on, or reject) all the ceremonies we had seen and heard and read about, most of which are based in religious tradition.

At the end of that wedding-chore week in late July, Adam and I went to the hotel where most of the guests would be staying to ask if we could reserve a space for a hospitality room. They sent us down a long hall to take a look at the room we would use; it was disappointingly sterile, a conference room with fluorescent lights. Can't we get some armchairs and side tables in here, I wanted to know; isn't there some extra upholstered furniture we could arrange in a loose approximation of a living room? Because that is what I had pictured, a living room into and out of which would flow this huge extended group I thought of as family; our friend Ozzie would pass my uncle Dave at the door; Adam's cousin Rena would pour a drink for my father's aunt Virginia. On the way back down the hall to the front desk, I fantasized that our wedding guests would fill not just the sixty rooms we had reserved, but the entire hotel. I pictured all their doors open to one another and inviting, I pictured them watching each other's kids at the pool, I pictured them gathered in the lobby planning their sightseeing for the day. My sister Sady was going to make a guide of the region suggesting ways for guests to fill their time between events; we were spreading the festivities over a long weekend, Friday through Monday. Sady was going to list all our favorite shops and restaurants and describe the local historic and scenic spots worth visiting; her boyfriend Paul would write about area swimming holes, in case the weekend was Virginia hot. So I pictured our guests mulling over these lists. And then I pictured them taking over these places, filling the whole town. Back in the car again, driving down the streets of my home town toward the next errand, I fantasized that in one month every car we passed, every face we saw when we looked out our windows, would be theirs.

Trying to explain the resurgence of interest in church weddings, one article posits that couples "instinctively seek a sense of continuity with the past." They aren't "interested in starting a new book; [they want] to provide the 20th or 30th chapter of a book that has been unfolding over centuries." That explains why you would want to marry, say, in the church your parents married in, wearing your grandmother's dress, using the exact vows your ancestors used. But it doesn't quite explain our wedding or even that of my sister or Adam's brother. We weren't trying to duplicate or carry on experiences remembered from our childhoods or reminisced about by our grandparents. We weren't trying to have our parents' weddings. Adam's parents were married in a subdued Orthodox ceremony with only immediate family, in the rabbi's study; they were keeping a low profile lest they imply that his mother converted *in order* to marry. Her new mother-in-law then gave a tea at her house following the ceremony. My parents married in "The Temple," the Hebrew Benevolent Congregation, an old, wealthy Atlanta Reform synagogue. Rabbi Rothschild, who married them, had known my mother as a child; she remembers hearing his sermons on civil rights (this was the temple that white supremacists bombed in 1958). My father, though he admired his politics, thought Rabbi Rothschild was "cold," perhaps because he was entirely lacking in the boisterous affectionate ethnicity that characterizes Daddy's Sephardic relatives. Their wedding was, in fact, as culturally Protestant as a wedding in a Jewish synagogue could be: no huppah, no ketubah, and for the reception, an elegant luncheon at the new downtown Hyatt Regency. My father's Mediterranean Jewish family was not as thoroughly assimilated as Atlanta's German Reform Jews; as a nod to Sephardic tradition, my mother made sure the Hyatt served rice instead of potatoes.

Our huppahs, our ketubahs, the whole arc of our ceremonies, these didn't come from our parents, they didn't even come naturally. When it was time for Amy and me to plan our Jewish weddings, we had to *research* Jewish weddings. She added a colored sash to her white dress to honor her Sephardic heritage, not because as a child she had seen many Sephardic brides in colorful dresses, but because as a bride she had read about them. She and our aunt Leslie both had a mikveh, a ritual bath, before their weddings; neither of them had had one before or has had since.

No one danced at my parents' wedding; no one danced at Adam's parents' wedding. But at his brother Josh's wedding, Adam tried to get everyone to dance the *hora*. The leader of the rock-and-roll band said, yes, he thought they could play "Hava Nagila," and Adam scurried about under the big reception tent trying to round up dancers and chair lifters. Up, awkwardly, went the bride and groom, and we began: we bounced them about over our heads, and danced in a circle around them. But like the band, we knew only how to begin; halfway through, we weren't altogether sure what to do next.

With great strain and effort we set these Jewish weddings in motion, as with great strain and effort we lifted those chairs and tried to follow the music. We wanted to dance this dance that harkened back to a tradition we never really had, a tradition we'd experienced more in movies than in life. It's not just Jews who try to summon some ethnic spirit into their celebration, either; at the reception of two dear friends, after their Greek Orthodox wedding, the murmur went forth for a bit of Greek dancing. This reception was in an officers' club in D.C.; the bride's father was an air force general. The room was the equivalent of a military dress uniform— elegant, bright, and a bit stiff; it was full mostly of white American Protestants, and, like the groom and his family, long-assimilated Irish Catholics. It turned out that exactly two people knew how to dance "Greek." The rest of us stood in a circle staring at the feet of a friend of the bride's mother, trying to make our feet do what hers did. We didn't even attempt to get the arms right. As an expression of joy, it was as far from spontaneous as you can imagine.

At a wedding between a bride of Hindu origin and a groom

(my cousin) of Jewish origin—neither of whom is religious—the bride's family transformed an Indian restaurant in a suburban New Jersey strip mall into a Hindu ceremonial space. At the *mandap*, the structure under which the bride and groom wed, the priest directed the proceedings in Sanskrit, Gujarti, and English, after explaining to us all that the traditional ceremony had been condensed from four days to one hour. The guests followed along from an elaborate tassled program embossed in red and gold; it had an Indian look about it, but it was a careful English explication of each symbol and ritual of the complicated ceremony. It wasn't just the non-Indian guests and the willing but untutored groom who needed guidance, though; the priest gently coached the bride on how to feed sweets to her groom and how to walk with him around the *agni*, the ceremonial fire, and even instructed her parents on when and how long to shower the couple with rice and flowers.

Protestants are working hard at their weddings too. I have been to many weddings that take place, not where the bride and groom, or even their parents, actually live, but in picturesque little American towns with perfect colonial, white-spired churches, never before attended by the couple in question. The solemn ceremonies are followed—depending on the image the couples have of their heritage—by an elegant reception at a country club overlooking a lake, or by supper at long tables in a social hall.

In all of these cases, bride and groom were not continuing a tradition, they were stealing from one. They were looking back beyond their parents, or even grandparents, to the kind of celebration *they imagined* their ancestors had. Why? What was it about that imagined time that they yearned for?

It was, I think, a sense of community. The element that links all the weddings I have described, all the weddings I have attended, is travel. Frequently the bride, the groom, the officiant, and the guests all must travel to the wedding site; no one lives there. There's an old piece of doggerel concerning the best day of the week on which to marry:

> Wed on Monday, always poor,
> Wed on Tuesday, wed once more,
> Wed on Wednesday, happy match,
> Wed on Thursday, splendid catch,
> Wed on Friday, poorly mated
> Wed on Saturday, better waited.

Today it's incredible to imagine wedding on Wednesday, unless it be a quiet matter in front of a judge—how could the guests possibly make it? People are no longer growing up and marrying in one community; we spread out. We make connections based on interests in college and try to maintain those friendships after we all disperse; or we try to keep our connections with childhood friends who have moved away. We Americans no longer simply connect with whatever community we have physically around us. We live our lives in the belief that our friends and loved ones can come from different backgrounds, that what connects us to them should be likemindedness, not likebloodedness or proximity. And yet when we wed, we seem to yearn for a sense of cohesion, of unity, of community.

The wedding is the one time in our lives when we get to have that community. In our fantasy town from an imagined past, all our family and all our friends would be just down the street. For one thrilling weekend, for the wedding weekend, they actually are. They all shop in the same shops and eat at the same restaurants, they all drive down the same roads. That's why we made our wedding last four days: we wanted to live in that fantasy town for as long as possible. And for our fantasy community, we created a fantasy celebration, fantasy rituals, from bits of ritual we knew and had read about. It was "Jewish" in our case because Jewish was familiar; it was a cultural heritage to which we had easy access.

This past that we wanted to return to never actually existed. That cozy shtetl community we seemed to yearn for would, I am certain, feel incredibly stifling to us if we lived in it. In Anatevka, the fictitious space of *Fiddler on the Roof*, everyone knows everyone else's business, everyone lends a hand, everyone sings in harmony at the wedding, which everyone in the town attends. But if it were a real town, and not a Broadway fantasy, the barrier between the men and the women that crumbles at the end of the wedding, to allow them, against Orthodox law, to dance together, would instead have stood firm. If we were required to have the religious components in our ceremony that "matched" the cultural components—if I had to circle Adam seven times, if we both had to remain silent throughout the ceremony, but for nine Hebrew words—we would have had a civil ceremony instead. We could not have endured the sexism of the Jewish ceremony in its pure state. Occasionally friends of ours are forced to make this choice; they can't bend their religious ceremony to their true beliefs, and instead have to take it or leave it. When they have taken it, the results have been, to me, painful. Adam and I have sat uncomfortable in our pew knowing for certain that the bride and the groom did not mean what they were saying and did not believe what they were hearing the officiant say. How can they be taking this seriously, we wonder, appalled, as the priest intones, "As the church is subject to Christ, so let wives also be subject in everything to their husbands." How can they feel sanctified—or even married—by words like these? But, then, how can they not, since they chose to wed this way, since they asked us to witness this wedding?

We were lucky; we didn't have to choose between strictly religious traditional or strictly secular modern. We could approximate an Old World sense of community without Old World strictures. We were free to have the kind of wedding we wanted.

Describing a California wedding between a Jew and a Presbyterian, Sara Bershtel and Allen Graubard, authors of a book on being Jewish in America, write:

> The ceremony is deliberately made up of traditional elements, bits and pieces of religion and culture, and it is the presence of these elements, given by the tradition, that provokes talk of revival [of religion among assimilated Jews]. But, in truth, the actual elements matter less than the fact that they can be chosen without regard to religious laws or cultural coherence, and combined into an individually constructed design.

In our ceremony, as we discussed with Rabbi Serotta that day in July, we would not speak of God, except in a few ritual Hebrew blessings. In our ceremony, though traditionally only the groom gives a ring, we would both give rings, after each one had made its way from the back of the room up to the huppah through the hands of our guests. In our ceremony we would rewrite the *sheva b'rachot*, the seven blessings: instead of praises of God chanted by the rabbi, they would be reminders of the blessings of our lives read aloud by our family and friends. We would write our own vows (vows are not part of the traditional Jewish wedding) and bring them into the ceremony as a *tosefet ketubah*, an addendum to the marriage contract. At the end of the ceremony we would stomp on the glass together. According to Bershtel and Graubard, Adam and I didn't choose a Jewish wedding at all. In its embrace of freedom and individuality, its use of half-remembered, half-invented ethnic heritage, our wedding was "not primarily a Jewish event: it [was] a modern—and above all, a modern American—event."

As Americans we have lost the tight bonds of Old World European Judaism. In fact, all of us, all Americans, are free and mobile; in this country, most of us believe on some level that to grow up is to move away from home. And all of us suffer the loss of a built-in sense of community, even if we remember such a community only from the movies. We pay for our freedom in phone bills and airline tickets and sheer time spent traveling; we pay for it every time we think, with a sigh, wouldn't it be great if we could invite this couple (who live in London) and that couple (who live in San Francisco) to dinner together at our house?

Having the built-in sense of community, living in a real Anatevka, would cost us our freedom, and we're not willing to give that up. We actually liked the idea of *choosing* a rabbi. He's not the one who happens to live down the street, happens to have been hired by the local synagogue. We asked him to marry us not because we had to, but because we admired his belief system, because he was a respected friend of a friend we respected, because we knew that, during the days of apartheid, he refused to use South African gold for his wedding bands.

Rabbi Serotta would be the rabbi in our fantasy community. For one weekend, he could be. For four days, the faces that populated our daily lives could be the faces only of people we loved. And with the help of a seating chart, for one night, the couple from London and the couple from San Francisco could be neighbors.

The Jewish groom-to-be in his Orioles cap tried to bond with his temporary rabbi through a common love of baseball, that most American of games. It was the picture of assimilation. Not of a Jew trying to assimilate Americanness, but of an American trying to figure out whether and how he can assimilate Judaism into his secular, progressive, universalist view of the world. Could he re-create that sense of community, of shared purpose, that he finds in a ballpark, when, one month later, he gathered his friends and family—his community—for the only time ever in one physical space, in a lecture hall in a Virginia museum? Would this rabbi help him turn them into a village, make them feel as if they had traditions, as if they were participating in a ritual so old as to be eternal? Up until the ceremony, Adam had not decided whether to cover his head as we wed; I was not, after all, wearing any marker of my Judaism. But he paused at the last minute, just as we were about to enter the hall behind my parents and his parents, took a kippah out of the boxful our rabbi had brought, and put it on.

9

Our Place at the Table

When we arrived at my parents' home in Virginia a week before the wedding, I started to cook. I was making food for an open house we had planned for guests coming into town on Friday night. There would be a large table each of sweets and savories, from 6 P.M. to midnight at my parents' house, so that whenever guests arrived and however much dinner or dessert they were in the mood to eat, they would be satisfied. I planned the menu, replenished my parents' supply of flour and butter and yeast, and set to work.

Everybody said I was crazy to cook, that I should just enjoy the week ahead, rather than spend it working. Adam couldn't decide whether I was motivated more by my martyr complex or by my desire to show off. But I felt I needed to do it. That week, people around the country were making an effort for us: working extra hours so they could leave their jobs early on Friday, buying or trying on the clothes they would wear, planning, packing, pacifying their carbound kids. They were wrapping presents for us, composing toasts about us, coming to celebrate us. I couldn't imagine simply enjoying it all as if that were my due. I wanted to work equally hard for them; I wanted to feel I had *earned* the trouble my guests were going to.

It wasn't just a need to reciprocate, though. I felt somewhat unsure of my role as bride. I didn't know how well I fit it. But I was comfortable in the role of chef and hostess; I knew I could play them well. When I look back now at that week's to-do lists, Monday through Friday, what strikes me is how familiar are the food and kitchen elements and how unfamiliar the rest. Almost every non-cooking item was something I hadn't done before and would never do again: "talk through vows," "check seating chart," "call Josh re: kiddush cup"; work in the kitchen was by contrast soothingly routine. The dip of pastry brush in butter, the scrape of spoon against spoon, the plop of filling on filo dough—all these things make me feel secure, in control, focused. The brightly lit aisles of a grocery store, any grocery store, fill me with calm.

The kitchen is a world in which I'm in total control, a world in which I feel good about myself. Food is my job at home in Albany, and I'm obsessive about it. When I come back home to Adam after a week in Virginia without him, I go straight to the refrigerator, where I almost always become incensed. "There's *pie* in here!" I'll exclaim, in the same tone of voice in which another person might say, "There's a *mouse* in here!" Meaning that in my absence he had failed to eat the last of the apple pie I had baked.

"Oh yeah. How'd I forget about that?"

"You never look in the refrigerator."

"That's true," he'll say, amused. I issue a series of instructions on my way out the door—how to thaw the potato-oat bread, that there's chicken broth and tortellini in the freezer for soup, and please eat the leftover broccoli-white-wine pasta—but he never follows them when I'm gone. For one thing, when I'm away, people feel sorry for him and invite him over for dinner. They forget that he managed to feed himself quite well before I entered his life, and they don't understand that, even if he didn't know spaetzle from a spatula, he'd be happy to eat McDonald's for a change.

For another thing, he's just not in the habit of looking in the fridge; I always do it for him. "Wait!" I cry at lunchtime, and he, pot in one hand and bright orange package of ramen noodles in the other, lifts his face to me, resigned. "There are leftovers in the fridge!" Sometimes he even pokes his head around the door of my study to ask, "What do you want me to eat for lunch?" The leftover creamy garlic linguine, of course—don't even think of eating ramen. Or, please get rid of the Chinese take-out—it's taking up room in my fridge.

My fridge. My pantry, my flour, my bread bowl, my pie plate, my vegetable drawer. Adam resists my culinary authority by ceding to it without struggle (thereby implying that food isn't important enough to argue about) and by refusing to be impressed by it. He knows that I am a good cook, is proud that I am, I think, but is therefore completely unmoved when—*voilà!*—I produce a flawless hollandaise. Did anyone actually believe I might not? I can please him with food, but I can't impress him with it.

Adam has his own areas of expertise, too. He keeps the car in good order, he keeps the snow plowed, he plants and tends the vegetable garden. He fixes the plumbing when it breaks, builds the furniture we need, installs electrical outlets, occasionally adds whole rooms to the house.

Wait, you say, there's something familiar about this division of labor, something I just can't put my finger on . . . OK. We know. It's straight out of a social anthropologist's report: "Food is a female concern," writes Margaret Visser, for instance. "Women gather food, shop, choose what is to be eaten, and cook it." Or a social critic's: "What is surprising," muses Jeremy MacClancy, "is that, in our post-industrial society where much of the economics underpinning this conventional separation of the sexes no longer holds good, most women still do the shopping, cooking, and clearing up." That's right, Adam and I are certifiably retrograde. It's embarrassing. And it gets worse: I write the thank-you notes, make or buy and wrap the gifts, sort the mail. He drives everywhere we go together, programs the VCR, pays the bills. He pays attention to our mutual funds. I am aware that we have some. I plan our cultural outings. He is aware that we have some.

The gender typing is not quite absolute, but the fact that he cleans the bathroom is poor consolation for a couple determined to be feminist, yet somehow destined to embody a division of labor straight out of the 1950s, when, as the historian Harvey Levenstein notes, "the competent housewife in her kitchen seemed well-nigh ubiquitous." I guess *destined* is not really the right word. Was I born with an innate ability to cook? Was Adam born with an innate ability to . . . do whatever it is he does? Probably not. Probably we each started with some natural aptitude, which combined first with vague social pressure and then with the drive we both had to master the roles we were given.

Is it too late to undo all that? The thing is, though we don't like the traditional way in which our labor is divided, we do like the fact that it is divided. We like being sure of our roles. We never have to argue about who's going to the grocery store or who's going to shovel snow off the porch steps, never hesitate about who sits where when we get in the car. And because we each take full responsibility in our separate realms, the flour canister is always full and the oil in the car has always been checked; nothing slips through the cracks. My image of myself as a complete, capable grownup requires that I be able to fix a leaky faucet; I can't, and will probably never learn to because Adam already can, has the tools, and—by golly, there he is, leaning over the sink in question. I could try to get him to teach me how, and he would probably be willing, but he'd be impatient with my clumsiness, and I'd be so irritated by his impatience that I would be absorbed more in it and in my irritation than in wrenches and washers. The next time a faucet leaked, I would still have no idea what to do.

As far as I can tell, this is how it's going to be. I will never be a complete, capable grownup. But I console myself with the thought that, since we've divided everything up, at least there's one complete, capable grownup *between us*.

In fact when we were at home in Virginia the week before the wedding, Adam did fix the leaky faucet. I think it was on that trip that he fixed the door to the second oven, too, which for years had crunched and whined as it opened, and refused to close completely. Meanwhile I was humming along, in a slight, happy panic, with butter melting in the microwave, bar cookie crust baking in the oven, onions simmering on the stove. Feeling like we were grownups, ready for a grownup thing like marriage.

Once or twice, as I was cooking for my guests, it occurred to me that they weren't really my guests at all. My parents and Adam's parents were the hosts that weekend, not me: they were the ones spending enormous sums, they were capably and generously planning for the welcome and entertainment of the guests. Saturday night there would be a picnic and contradancing at my parents' house with food from a local Mexican joint; Sunday morning a good friend had invited everyone to a brunch in our honor; Sunday evening was the actual catered affair; and Monday my parents would be cooking pancakes and pouring juice for anyone who needed a few more calories on the way out of town. Everyone, in other words, would be well fed. So why did I have to bother? Partly because I didn't feel I deserved our parents' effort and expense any more than I deserved that of hard-traveling friends and family; I wanted to contribute to the cause, if not in money then in sweat.

But my need to cook that week may also have come from a need to usurp my parents' role as hosts, to maintain authority at my wedding, an event in which tradition and the flow of funds clearly indicated that I was not the authority, that I was the child. I was not just reassuring myself that I was a competent grownup, but making sure my parents knew it too.

The kitchen was the place to do it, because the kitchen was where I grew up. I started as a child by snapping beans and tearing lettuce, helping my mother unload the groceries, carrying cheese and crackers to the living room from the metal-edged yellow Formica table where we had arranged them. I remember clearly when my older sister and I started to help serve the formal dinners, and then when we first served them by ourselves while one or the other parent cooked, and then when, one evening, Mom had drunk too much before dinner and told us gaily that we would have to steam the broccoli. And so we did. And later I began to make Toll House cookies on my own, till I became the one in the family who baked the cookies, and then the one who made the chocolate mousse, and assembled the baklava, and baked the rolls.

The one who cooked, as if there could be only one. But that's a little bit how families work, I guess, as well as couples: we establish roles for ourselves and each other, for simplicity's sake, for the ease of not deciding anew each time who does what. And also so we have a clear and definable sense of ourselves: what we can do, what people expect us to be able to do, goes a long way toward constructing who we think we are. My sisters and my parents are all good cooks and they all cook regularly, but ask them who is the one who cooks and they will name me.

I took the role to heart. My sophomore year in college I left the dorms and rented an apartment partly for want of a kitchen. And a year and a half after I graduated from college, when Adam and I finally got to live alone together (first we had lived with his parents, then with his brother at the farm), I was thrilled because it meant not having to share a kitchen. Sure, I was pleased to have privacy, but since we had always had our own bedroom, and we had always been able to shut the bathroom door, this new, thrilling privacy for me boiled down to, well, boiling whatever I wanted. I cooked and I cooked. I taught myself to bake breads and cakes, make jam, can tomatoes; I simmered twelve quarts of chicken stock at a time; I shucked, blanched, scraped, and froze bushels of corn; kneaded, rolled, and stuffed pounds of pasta. When I went home to visit my parents, I hungered to take over in their kitchen. I would cluck with exasperation at the three open pickle jars on three different shelves in the fridge, or the carrots rotting in the back of the vegetable crisper. I would take over the shopping and the cooking for dinner—my parents were working, I told Adam, and I had free time, why shouldn't I help out? Partly I *was* just being the good girl I had always been, but also, slyly, stealthily, I was being a grownup in my parents' kitchen. Maybe I was even trying to be more grownup than they.

But now, just as in my childhood when they entertained and I served, they were throwing a big party, spending lots of money, taking the week off from work to prepare to host. They were, I knew, great hosts. So what was I? What was my role? Pampered daughter? Beloved bride? That's why I stood aproned in my parents' narrow yellow and white kitchen, five years after setting up a kitchen of my own, one week before my wedding, trying to fit an entire patisserie's worth of baking around dress fittings and meetings with the caterer and the massage my sisters had scheduled for us. Trying to act organized and decisive and creative and competent. Trying to act in charge.

Food is love. That's what my family would say with a shrug at our dinner table when someone was pressing seconds on someone else. We were making fun of our obsession with food, of the importance we accorded it. But there is something about food, in most cultures, that gets down to the core—the guts, shall we say—of human interaction. It's a basic necessity, yes, even "the great necessity to which we all submit," as Margaret Visser asserts, but who says we have to submit to it together? And yet we feel sorry for people we see eating alone, we expect families to eat at least one meal a day together, and we suffer hunger for hours in order to wait to eat with company. Company, companion—from the Latin for people "with whom we share bread." Food is part of our life rituals: we bring food to a family in mourning and we bring food to the parents of a newborn. And it's part of our language of love: Jeremy MacClancy points out that "we hunger for love, feast our eyes, eat out our hearts, and suffer devouring passions." Unpleasant people are unpalatable, boring ones are insipid; lovely people are sweet, and we savor their company. We give chocolates to our spouses and chicken soup to sick friends; we go out to nice restaurants on first dates, and, if those go well, proceed to candlelit dinners at home.

There was love in the food I made that week. My need to make it may have come from other, more selfish impulses, but in the food itself there was much love. The rugelach, for instance, I chose because my father had told me recently how much he liked them. And I made lemon-poppyseed pound cake because my mom has a thing for lemon—and for butter. The pecan squares were for both of them, walnut-eschewing southerners that they are.

And I made bourekas in honor of my beloved paternal grandfather and that whole Sephardic side of the family. Bourekas are savory pastries stuffed with—in my family's Alabama version, via (Turkish) Rhodes via Spain—either potato and cheese or eggplant and tomato. I remember being little and lining up at the counter with my cousins in Alabama, awaiting instruction from Granddaddy, who was in charge then as I was now. I remember wanting to do my part well (was it rolling or stuffing or folding or sealing?) so Granddaddy would be pleased with me, and I remember checking my work against my cousins', who were younger than I but saw Granddaddy more often and were better at making bourekas. And I remember all that pressure or anxiety or competition or whatever it was disappearing when I bit into a first-batch boureka, and it was too hot, and too hot for my cousins too, but it was delicious and we were eager and our eagerness made Granddaddy giggle. And then we felt like a team, and we piled up those bourekas and were proud of our work.

So the bourekas were for Granddaddy, though he wasn't there. Because he wasn't there. But even food that wasn't about or for someone in particular had people connected to it. The cream cheese brownies—I didn't exactly make them *for* Adam, but I knew they would make him happy. The same went for the almond biscotti and Adam's mom. And the reason only one of my savories contained meat—the chicken and pecan pesto salad sandwiches on tiny soft rolls—was so there would be only one thing Aunt Ruth and Aunt Gita, who keep kosher, couldn't eat. I knew, as I spread a mixture of smoked salmon, cream cheese, horseradish, and dill on more of those tiny rolls, that Adam's dad would love them. I had to call my friend Mary Hill for the roll recipe; it is her mother's and I invariably misplace it, and she invariably reads it to me, cheerfully, when I call for help. The filo turnovers stuffed with goat cheese remind me of my sister Amy, who ate cheese pastries called tiropites when she lived in Greece. My friend Danny, a food-loving vegetarian, was in my mind when I grilled eggplant to layer with fresh tomato slices on rosemary focaccia. And dividing the egg mixture for the potato, pepper, and caramelized onion frittatas reminded me of my friend Lena, with whom I had made rolled frittatas for a crowd the year before.

I wanted to give the people I loved delicious things to eat, to show them how much I cared about them, thought about them, wanted them to be happy and satisfied. Food is love—I was giving them that. Does that love get all mixed up with pride and power and the need to please? Of course. Food is love, but love is complicated. Anyone whose child comes home and declares she's a vegetarian knows that. "Power struggles between men and women are frequently expressed through the medium of food," writes Visser. "Children . . . can cause a flurry of parental concern by refusing to 'eat properly.' The eating disorder called anorexia ('not stretching forth the hand and taking' in Greek) usually includes love-refusal as part of its original strategy." A child's new-found vegetarianism is upsetting far beyond the degree to which it complicates the grocery list; it can feel like a criticism, a rejection of love, even when it isn't meant that way.

My mother, who cooked the evening meal in our family, seemed to have little ego invested in it; she seemed not to mind handing over the baking duties to me or hearing a new dish critiqued (I say "seemed" only because, having the opposite attitude, I can hardly believe hers). For my father, on the other hand, cooking was an expression of love and personality; it was an event. My mother was the one who cooked the balanced meals; my father's specialties were onion rings, cream of mushroom soup, fried Chinese scallion bread, pecan-crusted fried chicken, french fries—foods that please; when he was cooking, he never made us eat kid-resistant foods like peas. And yet he *was* putting pressure on us, unintentionally, by making foods that were so clearly treats, gifts for his children. How could we reject such gifts, whether we were hungry or not? How could we possibly appreciate them enough? We would be late for Sunday school because he wanted to make us pecan waffles, sausage with a sweet cornmeal crust, homemade glazed donuts, cornbread, pancakes. We loved the food; we loved him; we hated to be late. We had no choice. Daddy in his maroon bathrobe dusted with flour, saying "these pancakes are so light they're going to fly away" or "wait, don't eat these, they're not that good," "But, Daddy—" "No, no, I'm going to do them right." "Look at all the biscuits left—what, you didn't like them?"

At that point he was kidding, and we kidded back. But we *were* afraid of hurting his feelings. So for years we acted out a kind of culinary farce: he, though he hated eggs, made us a sweet custardy concoction called Wellskringle for each of our birthdays, and we, though it made us gag, ate it smilingly, year after year.

I don't remember which of us daughters told him the truth first, but I do know we were all long out of the house when she did. He laughed about it, and mulled ruefully over the tangled mix of guilt and obedience and the desire to please that was prompted by what he had intended as an expression of love. For my wedding shower my mother-in-law instructed everyone to bring a recipe, and my father sent Adam the recipe for Wellskringle, along with a humorous introduction describing how his search for the perfect break-fast food to serve his picky children ended in the discovery of this dish.

> Without fail their response was touching. I remember watching Kate's eyes get big, and—I don't think I'm imagining this—moisten, and she would be absolutely speechless. Actually, I suspect that she got a lump in her throat which made it hard for her to speak or eat, since there was always plenty left over. The odd thing is that normally our dog, Joe, would eat the breakfast left-overs, but believe me, Adam, when I tell you that some-how he must have sensed how special Wellskringle was to my girls, because that dog wouldn't eat a bite of their special breakfast meal.

It was a funny piece of self-mockery, but it reminded me all over again of the cycle that began in love and giving and ended, through fear of hurting his feelings, in lies and awk-wardness. And all this swirling about a dish as simple (I real-ized as I read the recipe for the first time) as undercooked cream puff pastry. That's all it was. Piped into tiny blobs and baked until the insides dried, it would be yummy.

My father sent this recipe to Adam and not to me because, in accordance with our brilliantly original role division, Adam is the brunch cook in our family, just as my father is in mine. And don't think there wasn't a bit of competitive french toast making when Adam and my father first met. But Adam doesn't normally let his feelings get all mixed up in his cook-ing; that's what my father and I do. We are not alone, either: many of the recipes I received for the wedding shower had to do more with feelings than with food. One aunt gave me the recipe that was used for her wedding cake. One cousin trans-planted to Boston from New Orleans sent a jambalaya recipe.

One friend wrote me a long story about how she learned to cook as a young housewife, and gave me the chicken soup recipe that became her children's and her grandchildren's favorite. A neighbor gave me a bit of doggerel called "Contentment by the Cupful," a recipe for a happy marriage. A heaping cup of happiness, two of love and caring, one of understanding, one of joyful sharing—that sort of thing. I thought to myself, Why do people always write recipes with exotic, hard-to-find ingredients?

I didn't say it, though; I smiled and thanked her for the sentiment. Which is easy with people you don't know that well. With people you love and who love you, the question is, can you be grateful for the gift and still confess that you don't really want it? Can you say, "Daddy, thank you so much, but this stuff is pretty disgusting. Make me some of your featherweight pancakes next time"? I'm trying to learn from Adam's no-nonsense example; I've gotten to the point where I can admit I don't really like french toast at all, no matter who makes it, but I still feel vaguely rejected when *he* doesn't want to eat what *I* make. Rejection of food can be interpreted throughout the world as a wounding insult, but I try to tell myself that I am not in a Bedouin tent trying to read the intentions of a stranger. Adam loves me; he just doesn't like sweet potatoes. Food is a powerful *metaphor* for love, I tell myself, it isn't *really* love. I'm not entirely convinced: I still need praise for the food I make, I still feel compelled to remark casually to Adam after a dinner party, "I thought those soufflés turned out well, didn't you?"

Making bourekas is a long, labor-intensive task; I looked at the clock in a panic and realized that they all had to be shaped and baked within the next two hours if I was going to get to my dress fitting on time. My shoulders tensed as I tried to pick up the speed a bit; I think it was the slap of rolling pin on Formica that brought my father and my older sister into the kitchen. He had been cleaning the clutter from his study; she had been sewing our huppah. "Need some help?" asked my father, and Amy looked at me too and waited for my answer. I had thought of all this cooking as my project, my contribution, mine. I looked at the clock: I needed some help. "Yeah," I said. My father and my sister were old hands at boureka making; they learned it from Granddaddy just as I had. So when they said, "What can we do?" I said, "OK, you stuff" and "you can seal" and handed them the two spoons and the fork and off we went.

I bring Adam his dinner as he sits on the living-room sofa; the next day, he asks me what I want him to eat for lunch; in Virginia, my mom feeds me (what once was) my favorite meal; the next day, I urge my father to make his Sunday biscuits not from Bisquick but from scratch. Even within one couple, within one family, the emotions, the history, the rituals around food are as rich and multilayered as the smells that emerge from it. Even within one couple, within one family, the roles we take in the kitchen and at the dinner table tell us something about the roles we take in our relationships. That's why Adam and I are so uncomfortable about the gendered split of cooking and eating at our house—of everything we do—because, again, what you and the world think you can do is so crucial to who you think you are. But cooking and eating especially, because they are the central rituals, from nursing to the nursing home. We take certain roles around these rituals, just as we take certain roles in our relationships, our families, and adjusting those roles—taking charge in your parents' kitchen, or becoming a child in it again after long being a grownup in your own—can be hard, hurtful, and full of meaning.

If dinner with Adam and breakfast with my parents can be so rich with significance, a feast that brings two families and their friends together must be more than simply a joyous celebration. It weds hosts and guests in a complex ritual of connection and hospitality, of giving and taking, of fulfilling or forgoing family and social roles. It tells us where we fit in our community: child or grownup, guest or host, to put it at its simplest. That is why the wedding feast, which Carolyn Mordecai calls "the most universal feature of weddings" in her book on worldwide wedding customs, can be as significant a statement as the wedding—or even *the* significant statement of the wedding. Many cultures have special wedding foods: Armenians make an enormous saffron pilaf flavored with rosewater; Turks have a traditional wedding soup, dugun corbasi, made of meat and vegetables and flavored with egg-lemon sauce; many Arab peoples emphasize the sweetness of weddings with trays of pastries, nuts, and confections, especially candy-coated almonds. Norwegian weddings feature a tower of a wedding cake constructed of almond rings and decorated with sugary flowers, Norwegian flags, and a tiny bride and groom. The Ukrainian wedding cake, actually a loaf of bread called a korovai, is even more elaborate: to produce it, seven bridesmaids grind flour taken from seven different sources; every guest at the feast must taste it. Frequently too the point of wedding food is for it to be like everyday food, but more luxurious, to emphasize the special quality of the day. For wedding feasts in Bulgaria, for instance, the oven-baked stew called a guivech, normally vegetarian, would be enriched with lamb; the Chinese wedding banquet might simply have more, and more elaborate, courses than a normal meal.

It's not just what we eat that gives a wedding feast its meaning. Think of the shock value and the strategic brilliance of Petruchio's refusal to let Kate stay for her wedding feast in *The Taming of the Shrew*. Who gives the reception and who pays how much for it can be deeply significant; why else would so many people who'd never hired a caterer before hire one for a wedding? Who gets on the guest list for that reception can be just as momentous: the Trojan War began because the Greek goddess Eris, annoyed to be the only one in the Pantheon not to be invited to Thetis and Peleus's wedding, tossed the apple of discord in among the guests. As for the symbolism of who sits where at a wedding feast, Jesus (whose first public miracle was turning water into wine at a wedding) found the topic serious enough to contain a parable about humility. But you don't have to know Shakespeare or Greek mythology or the New Testament to know that who sits with the bride and groom and who sits with the drunken uncle mean something; that's why it's so hard to make a seating chart. Food is love, but love is complicated.

When guests started to arrive for the party Friday night, the wedding officially began. This was the first event on the long list we had sent to each out-of-town guest, this would be their first taste of the weekend. Half an hour before, there had been chaos—it happens before every party, no matter how much time you thought you had earlier when you looked up and the kitchen clock said noon. Half an hour before, my mother had searched the pantry for a silver serving platter and I had called to my sister from the bathroom to get the filo pastries out of the oven before they burned, and, Daddy, do we have enough ice? Finally the bourekas were piled on warming trays in the dining room, the pecan squares stacked artfully on a table in the living room: the food was ready. So I stood on the porch and watched the first cars pull up, one by one, into the long gravel area between the street and the front lawn I had played on as a child. Where I had fed my pet rabbit from my hand, twirled in a swing under a maple, climbed the windmill so I could perch with the members of my secret club on the green tin roof of the old washhouse. Engines were turned off, doors slung open, and the people who emerged framed by the field across the street had come from Boston or New York or Toronto or Atlanta. They were here at the site of my childhood to witness . . . my having grown up.

Because that's how I thought about getting married; it was about taking our place in a community of grownups, it was about not playing house, however skillfully, anymore, but living it for real. We'd joined the American community merely by deciding to wed. And we'd gathered our smaller, chosen community here together for one weekend. For the purpose, I believe, of officially taking our place in it. We had been gradually assuming our roles in the community for years, gradually changing in Albany from the Greenbergs' boy and his girlfriend to the grownup couple we were. We wanted this long wedding weekend—I wanted tonight's meal—to celebrate that fact, to solidify it.

I greeted our first guests and led them inside. This was the living room where, as a child, I had circulated with my tray among familiar and unfamiliar faces; this was the study where, in raucous party din, I had ladled strong punch into outstretched cups; this was the dining room where, with a ten-year-old's charm and confidence, I had coaxed shy guests to the buffet and entreated them to eat. Tonight I offered food to friends and family without the sense that I was acting, yet with a great feeling of confidence in my role—confidence enough to share it. I didn't have to be the only grownup, the way, playing house, the child taking the role of mom demands that all the other children be the kids.

I could be, wanted to be, one grownup among many. My father and my mother and my sisters and my husband-to-be greeted guests and chatted and hugged and poured drinks and handed out plates as one host, with one welcome. With shouts and hand signals and tugs on each other's arms we managed as a group to refill the buffet and keep an eye on the ice and gather the empty plates in the kitchen. Which meant that when I was crossing from the kitchen to the study, I had time enough to pause at the dining room table and bite into a boureka we had made. Granddaddy would have been proud: it was delicious.

10
Wedding

Waking up, part one: For the week before our wedding, we slept upstairs in my parents' house, on the futon in the TV room. Our "best woman," who had come from England, was sleeping in the next bedroom over, a few short steps and a thin door away. Around the corner was my parents' room; they left their door ajar because you have to go through their room to get to the upstairs bathroom. The arrangement, in other words, was wholly without privacy. It suited us, though, because it gave us something to complain about, and because it matched our sense that we were a public couple, not the kind that needed to come to whispered decisions in private, or spend every moment latched to one another.

A public couple, but still a couple, and as a couple we shared a bed. The idea that we would stay apart before our wedding made no sense to us: how were we supposed to sleep if not together? So we slept, together, wedged between the video collection, the window, and the wall, our skin alive with that extra awareness of one another that you get when sleeping in an unfamiliar bed. At home in Albany, we go to sleep touching, but separate at some point in the night, and only upon waking do we once again nudge our limbs toward one another. But here in my parents' home, we spooned more, curled ourselves up in a double fetus. Because we were wearing pajamas, which we never do in our own bed, and, I suppose, because my parents were in the next room, it felt like the intimacy of childhood, of innocence. Like children on a week-long summer sleepover, we were completely open to each other, completely in sync. Even our dreams began to merge. When Adam woke in the middle of the night to pee, I did too, and after a couple of nights, we started to follow one another to the downstairs bathroom so as not to bother my parents. The wedding week was spinning by; I can hardly say which night it was when on our barefoot journey, I said to Adam: "I dreamt the band didn't show Saturday night."

"That's OK," he said. "It rained."

Bed is where we are wedded. It is where love is most companionate and calm: in bed we share sheets and a quilt and the air that we breathe through the night. It is where love is most intimate and impassioned: in bed we have sex and darkness-aided discussions of our selves. It is where love is most protective and caring: in bed we tend each other's sickness, guard each other's sleep. Bed is where our love lives.

And where it will die. "Bridebed, childbed, bed of death," James Joyce calls it. I have a friend who has planned his escape from a car if it goes off a bridge and sinks in the water. Actually he has two plans, one for automatic windows and one for the kind you roll down. Drowning in the steel trap of an automobile is the thing that scares him most, and so he has forced himself to think it through, to strategize. I have also forced myself to face the worst: I have determined that if the tricks of time and nature do not grant me my fervent wish, and Adam dies before I do, I will not sleep alone that night. If we have children, I will sleep with all or one of them. Or maybe it will be my mother, one of my sisters, my aunt who lives only three hours away (I have imagined phoning her to ask; she would come). It's the thought of an empty bed, of a bed without Adam, coldly declaring its present and future without-Adam-ness that I can't stand. I will fall asleep from the exhaustion of sobs and hiccups and of trying not to cry every time I speak; I will wake and the body next to mine won't be Adam's and that will make me weep. But I won't be alone in our bed.

Waking up, part two: The summer was, when I look back, a long montage of wedding planning, except for one other sharp memory: that of losing our cat, Emmitt. Emmitt had found his way to our door two years earlier; believing ourselves to be frequent travelers and knowing my mother to be allergic to cats, we decided not to take him in. But my resolve to cart him off to the humane society lasted until he licked my eyebrows the night a visiting friend let him in to eat. He climbed into my lap, looking for some part of me to tend to. He found the little furry strips above my eyes, and, after several rough laps of the tongue, he curled up in my lap to sleep. At that point, he owned me. There's something solemn about having something sleep on you, perhaps because of the inherent stillness of the act—no loud noises, no sudden moves, or the seal is broken. First Emmitt approaches cautiously, negotiating the hills and valleys of my legs, hidden treacherously beneath a blanket. Then he picks a spot and kneads my thighs or belly or breasts as if I'm a beanbag chair to be molded into shape. Then he coils himself into bed, his paws sometimes tucked under, sometimes resting on his nose, covering his eyes. Though that first posture is defensive, as he sleeps, he stretches out, front legs perhaps draped across my arm, back legs splayed to the side. Sometimes he'll end up on his back, all four legs relaxed in midair, chin tipped back. At this point, I have to pee or I've read all the magazines within reach or I really should start supper. But I can't move. Although his sleeping on me theoretically gives me complete power over him, it actually renders me helpless: I find myself incapable of disturbing his sleep. I forgive him all the times he jumps on the kitchen counter or stretches out on a manuscript I'm editing. He trusts me enough to sleep on me—how many creatures can I say that about?—he trusts me as much as I trust my own bed. He relies on me to support his utterly vulnerable sleeping body. How can I not offer him back warmth, stability, and comfort?

One day late in the June before we married, Adam came inside to say that he had run over Emmitt. The cat must have been under the car; Adam felt the tire hit something as he started to back out and then saw Emmitt limp under the porch. We tried all day to coax him out; meanwhile we talked over what we were willing to spend at the vet's if we could get him there. We didn't believe Emmitt's life should be saved at any cost: we knew on some level that our love for this cat was misplaced. This is a creature we feed and play with and remove ticks from. He has a personality, but he's not a person. And sometimes when I come into the kitchen to find him, butt and tail in the air, licking some morsel in the sink, looking like a raccoon rooting through a garbage can, I think, What sort of madness is this pet thing? How could we explain this to visitors from Mars? But he *sleeps* on me. I refused to name a vet bill limit; I just said I would know when it was overstepped.

Finally, at eleven at night, I lured Emmitt out with food and cooing. He was frightened and favoring a leg, but he looked to be all right. The next morning, the vet fitted him with a fiberglass cast (a bargain at two hundred bucks), but back home, Emmitt simply could not figure out how to walk with it. He would try to stand and instead would stagger backward a few steps and flip over, a hilarious piece of slapstick that was all the funnier for being wordless—no curses, no apologies, no self-deprecating jokes to mar the elegance of the silent-film pratfall. We couldn't help giggling, but we were worried that he wasn't eating or drinking or using his litterbox because he couldn't stand up. The next day we finally held him up at his food and water, and he took a little, but the kitty litter was a no-go: he couldn't get simultaneous help and privacy.

When I called the next morning, the vet said, Sometimes it just takes a little time. The day after that, with Emmitt still falling over backward, I took him outside. I figured he couldn't run away and if I left him for a few minutes, he might gain the privacy he needed to get his intestinal tract going.

Half an hour later he was gone. We looked under the porch, and all around the house, and in the barns where he likes to hide and hunt. And we looked, shrugging as we went, through the nearest fields: this was a cat who couldn't do anything except fall over, so how far could he have gone? And if he were stuck somewhere, trapped by his cast, wouldn't he cry? I went to the grocery—we were having friends over for a barbecue—and came back hoping he'd be waiting on the porch. Our guests left for home after dark; still we expected Emmitt to return. We went for one last round of calling around the barns. We ripped off the boards from around the crawlspace under the porch. We woke up in the middle of the night and looked out the front door. No cat.

I think it was the next afternoon that I really believed he

was gone for good; I still didn't know how. Did coyotes come and get him in broad daylight? Did he get trapped somewhere? Die of thirst or a blocked colon? We decided that he must have had some internal injury the vet hadn't caught and had gone off to die.

I wept, on and off, for several days. And I hated going to bed at night, when the sadness of it just sat there in the darkness waiting to envelop me. Emmitt was a good cat, the first cat I'd ever had, and (I now realized) he represented a whole happy, domestic period in my life: the last two years with Adam, when we were well settled into our home, our friend Kyle was living in the upstairs half of the house, my first book was published. But I think if Emmitt had died of old age or been flattened by a passing car, I wouldn't have felt as awful as I did. It was the sense of responsibility—not so much leaving him outside, but being (surely) within reach of him while he suffered and died and not doing anything to help him. Couldn't I have taken his disappearance more seriously at first? Couldn't I have made the vet check the rest of him more carefully? Shouldn't I have taken him back to the vet when he wouldn't eat or learn to walk?

Even if I were guilty of no particular neglect, I was responsible for Emmitt—I was someone he trusted enough to sleep on—and Emmitt had suffered, alone, an unnatural death. I had not been able to protect him. The pain of that fact filled me with a flooding nausea; and the shame I felt at being so upset over the death of a pet made me even sicker. I was disgusted, but not particularly surprised, to note how quickly sentiment had overtaken my rational mind. But I was shocked at the other emotions in me: the anger and irritation I felt toward Adam. I had never really suffered pain before in Adam's company—nothing more serious than the after-effects of fights with my father or rejections from publishers—and I could hardly believe, now that I *was* upset, that he couldn't make everything all right. That he had not been able to protect me from even the smallest of life's tragedies. I realized I had come to trust him so utterly, to rely on him so completely, that I had shifted the responsibility of guarding me from pain and sadness from my own shoulders to his. I hadn't noticed as it happened; it was as if a secret substance had passed between us during seven years of sleep. Now I kept waiting for him to do something, to walk inside holding the sick but living cat and sing out, "Kate, I have a present for you . . ." Or even to find the cat's dead body, to find out what had happened. And he didn't.

Before we went to bed a week later, I was still glancing onto the porch hoping to see Emmitt's face. To get from the front door to our bedroom, I walked past his food and water; I still had not been able to throw away the kibble and wash the bowls. But as I lay in bed awaiting sleep, a plan for the next night's dinner party, not Emmitt's face, nudged its way into my thoughts. And sleep came more quickly than it had for a week; no cat stood in the way to trip it up.

The first thing I heard in the middle of the night was footsteps on the stairs and the door between Kyle's apartment and our kitchen opening. Kyle said, "Adam. *Adam.*"

Adam sat up fast. "What is it?"

"Emmitt's outside."

He was. Thin and skittish, he ran—gracefully, fast, despite his cast—back into the nearest cornfield when we came out. Any of us could have lured him back with food, I think, but Kyle and Adam let me do it. I walked out and placed the bowl in front of him, and watched him eat for a while before it occurred to me that I was supposed to pick him up and bring him inside.

Lying on top of Adam after sex, I hold my upper body away from his to study his face in the sunlight. His eyes are closed, and his face and hair, brows and lashes are all in shades of gold. Two or three long blond hairs straggle from his eyebrows. My arms locked under the warm weight of his shoulders, I bend down and carefully, dryly, lick his eyebrows smooth. This is what marriage is, I thought: grooming one another—you fold his cuffs back, he hooks the clasp on your necklace, you pick the hay out of his hair, he brushes the flour from your cheek—without comment, without flourish, almost without thought.

I judge a movie by its dialogue; the actual best pictures of the year, I believe, are the ones nominated for best screenplay. But some of my favorite scenes in movies full of great talk are the silent ones; two from the year before our wedding come quickly to mind. I loved the wordless final scene of *Big Night*, when Secondo reconciles with Primo not by talking through their issues, but by making him an omelet in the quiet of their restaurant kitchen, by eating with him. Toward the end of *Walking and Talking*, Amelia is driving while Andrew is sleeping; she nudges him awake, he steers as she grapples off her sweater, she tosses the sweater in his lap, he balls it up to use as a pillow and goes back to sleep. We have seen these two friends joke and talk and fight, but this twenty-two-second scene of silent, mutual aid and understanding is how we know they are meant to be together. Boyfriends and girlfriends, people on dates, fallers in love, they have words, they have quips and quarrels and crossword puzzles, they have confessions and confidences and codewords for sex. A couple meant for marriage has more than that: it has silence, a life outside of spoken language.

Thank goodness. Adam and I have said horrible things to each other, vicious things. But words, even ugly ones, eventually vanish. Sometimes it takes a little while. After a fight, our words can hang in the air like the acrid smell of a kitchen fire. I leave to run errands and, in the hour or so of pleasant interactions at the bank and the post office, my mood returns to its usual calm good cheer, but when I open my front door again and inhale, suddenly I remember: Oh, right, the flare-up. But somehow, at some point, the smoke clears, whether you open a window or not. I don't mean to say that words aren't important—how could I?—if my house smelled like that for days on end I would have to move out. Only that, as long as the fires are occasional, the air will clear in between. What's left is how close we sit to each other on the sofa in the evening, after the crossword puzzle has been tossed aside in frustration. What's left is handing over the shampoo in the shower, squeezing toothpaste on two brushes instead of one. What's left is a warm hand pulling a blanket up around cold shoulders in the night.

With my body, I thee worship.

Waking up, part three: Lying on my side I try to think what day it is, what I need to do. I shift, pull a knee up to my chest, shut my eyes. Adam, belly down, pushes his head under his pillows. I remember a fight and turn over onto my back, trying dimly to reconstruct it. I stretch my left leg, let my hip open up, and graze his left leg with my knee. After a second, I push my leg straight so my foot aligns with his, except that his is sole up, mine is sole down. In his sleep he flutters his toes a little in a caress. It had been a stupid fight; he had said unfair things, I had argued beyond reason. We had gone to sleep with our backs to each other. I can just see his chin under his pillow, and a dark soft spot of neck, utterly relaxed. I lie there, not wanting to get up while he sleeps. Suddenly his head pops up, hair in a static halo, to look at the clock. 8:46. He grunts and drops his head, this time on top of the pillows. I say, "I'm going to put the water on, do you want anything? Some tea?" He says, eyes closed, "Yeah. Why not?" I sit up, pulling my feet out of blanket heat and into bedroom chill. I pause to let my brain adjust to vertical, and I silently thank my bed. I never wake up angry; I know now, when my back is turned on Adam, simply to shut my eyes and wait for morning. The sooner silence and sleep take over, the sooner our ugly words and my fierce frustration evaporate, leaving only that part of us that cannot change to vapor, the weight and warmth of our two naked bodies in bed.

Weight and warmth and sleep: Emmitt's whole life, in other words. Maybe that's what we get from pets—a pure, silent relationship, communication that, without the fog of spoken words around it, seems clearer and truer than the kind we have with most humans. More communion than communication. What Emmitt understands are my smell, my caress, the sound of my digging into his dry food with a tin cup, a high-pitched sing-song call, and the fact that when he cries I open the door. It's a five-word language, incredibly simple, based on the grammar of dependence, responsibility, and trust that we have established.

And yet, I still use spoken words on him, superfluous though they are. "Emmitt," is meaningless to him; if he comes when I open the door and yell "Emmitt!" it's because he heard the door open. Kissy noises and a high-pitched "Heeeeeere kitty-kittykitty" fetch him far more quickly than the name we have given him. But I can't help talking to him, soothing him with the sound of my voice, which really means, I suppose, soothing myself. Maybe that's why we refer to words like *honey*, *sweet knees*, and *sugarlips* as "pet" names: they are as useless and as pleasurable as the names we call our pets.

Adam and I don't need to call one another by our real names, and we usually don't. We sign notes to one another ("Off to library. Back in an hour"), if we sign them at all, with "A" or "K"; we call each other "hon" or "babe." Those abbreviations, those pet names, are a way to erase names themselves, to erase the formal distance that stands between us. If I walked into the room where Adam was and I said, "Snoopy!" or "Chuck!" or "Tootsie!" he would know I was talking to him. I could be referring to no one else. From the other room I call out "Puppy?" and he answers "Yeah?" I am embarrassed to admit I call him Puppy; Puppy is not a clever nickname, a wordplay nickname, a nickname based on some sharp insight into Adam's character; it's about as intelligent as baby talk. But that's what nicknames are about: intimacy on the other side of language. An acknowledgment that what Adam is to me now is beyond "Adam."

It wasn't always like that. When I first started to fall for Adam, I couldn't stop talking about him, I couldn't keep that name, Adam, from coming out of my mouth. But then the closer we got, and the longer we were together, the less I used it. It was as if "Adam" were too small a term for Adam, too specific. It's the name he signs checks with, the name telemarketers use, the name other people call him. Slowly my names for him became more general—"my boyfriend," "my guy," "my honey." Though "my man" feels just a little too bluesy to pass my lips, I can see the pleasure in calling someone "my man" or "my woman": it gives you ownership over something universal, as if your particular someone were the incarnation of the very idea of man or woman. Universal and also extremely vague, of course. But that lack of specificity feels right too, as if I have given up on the idea of expressing Adam's Adamness or what his relationship is to me; people can simply think whatever it is they think when they hear the word "guy."

It is, again, the difference between day and night, between date and spouse. The falling-in-love days are when you want everyone to know him, understand him, appreciate him; the being-in-love nights are when you exist in the subconscious land below or beyond names. By day we wear highly specific identifying elements like jobs and clothes and names and all the words we say; by night we are a universal: two people in bed. In bed, I have never called Adam by his name. And I can never quite believe sex scenes in movies where a woman enunciates, "Oh, William!" in the throes of passion. It's unnatural. The name belongs way back in the "Can I buy you a drink?" part of the evening. Just as the postcoital scene with the sheet clamped firmly under the female's armpits makes no sense either: you cover your breasts only in the presence of people you don't have sex with—unless you're cold, in which case you pull your covers up to your chin.

Waking up, part four: Thunder like rifle shots behind the ear cracked us alert at 12:46. In one adrenalined instant I had jumped and thrown my arms around Adam, let go, and looked at the clock. "That was something," we agreed. Lying in bed trying to dissolve consciousness again, I thought, how odd to cling to Adam as if he could save me from *lightning*. He is stronger than I, warier, and more aggressive, but, let's face it, the margin of things he can save me from that I can't save myself from is slim: an improvised mugging, perhaps, general harassment of the single female. He is, as I am, merely a small, unarmed human, unaccustomed to violence—no match for a lightning bolt.

My protector against things one cannot be protected from. My guardian against lightning and floods and tornadoes, my vanquisher of pain and sorrow, sickness and death. I know he can't do any of it; he can't even promise me that he will outlive me, that he will be there in the night when I wake in fright. And yet, in that first, worst instant of fear, before reason can catch up, I believe that he can save me.

When did he come to mean safety? When did he come to be safer than bed and pillow and sleep itself? When he grew too large in my mind to fit into a name anymore, when he simply became what I rested on, what allowed my body to relax and lose for a few hours its guarded stance, its grip on the dangers of the day.

The room still flickered full of silver light every few seconds, but the storm had moved away, and the thunder had dulled to a rumble in the distance. He shifted back to his standard sleeping position, on his belly, outside arm around his pillow, inside arm at his side, palm up, so I, lying on my back, could hold his hand. He told a friend once, back in the early years of us, that he didn't like going to sleep unless he was touching some part of me, even if it was just my pinkie. Sometimes I hold his outstretched hand firmly; that night I just placed my fingertips there gently, enjoying the way, after a time, touch disappeared, and I couldn't tell where the edges were—where my fingers ended and his began.

At the end of the wedding week, we married. It was the marriage of two verbal people, and as such it was an unusually wordy affair, a statement composed of many statements. We had worked hard to get the words right: the early save-this-date letter, the invitation, the direction-and-instruction letter, the program explaining the ceremony, and, of course, the blessings and vows of the ceremony itself. The vows, which we had begun and then abandoned back in April, we finished tinkering with just two days before the wedding. We finally practiced them the day before the ceremony, during a stolen half hour in my mother's office.

> We promise each other: I will turn to you when I am in need, and care for you when you are.
> We promise each other: I will take strength from who you are, forgive who you are not, and remind you who you want to be.

   We promise each other: I will try to remember, whether
sunk in sorrow or distracted by the day-to-day, what I
feel at this moment—my sense of good fortune, my sheer
joy at being with you.
   We say to each other: Knowing my family and friends
surround me, knowing who I am and who I want to be—
with this strength and certainty I say to you: I have only
one life, and it is only so long, and I choose to spend it
with you.

It was the first time we read them aloud, and though
we stood amid fluorescent lights and stacks of folders and
particle-board furniture, I could not read them to Adam
without crying. I think they were good words, and said as
well as possible what we wanted to say. And I hope and
believe that they might last a while, too, in meaning.

The next day we said those same words, standing in front
of our rabbi under our huppah held up by our siblings. And
they felt right. But I think now that a lot of different words
would have worked, just as, if I called out "Pokey!" right now,
Adam (the least pokey human being I know) would answer
from the living room. It wasn't the words that wedded us: it
was hand gripping hand as we walked down the aisle; it was
shoulder touching shoulder as we read our vows; it was tears
and trembling lips. And it wasn't the words our friends said
that blessed us, it was their pushing themselves up from
their seats to say them, the catch in their throats, the shake
of their hands. Their bodies in that room on that day. And,
in the moment before we entered that room, their hushed,
weighty silence.

Sources

Ackerman, Diane. *A Natural History of Love*. New York: Random House, 1994.

Alighieri, Dante. *La Vita Nuova*. Translated by Barbara Reynolds. London: Penguin, 1969.

Barer-Stein, Thelma. *You Eat What You Are: People, Culture and Food Traditions*. Willowdale, Ont.: Firefly Books, 1999.

Bershtel, Sara, and Allen Graubard. *Saving Remnants: Feeling Jewish in America*. New York: Free Press, 1992.

Bride's All New Book of Etiquette. New York: Putnam/Perigee Books, 1994.

Brightman, Joan. "Why Hillary Chose Rodham Clinton." *American Demographics* 16, no. 3 (March 1994): 9.

Byfield, Ted, and Virginia Byfield. "Church Weddings May Be Back for Good Reasons." *Alberta Report Newsmagazine* 22, no. 40 (September 18, 1995): 39.

Clark, Charles S. "Marriage and Divorce." *CQ Researcher* 6, no. 18 (May 10, 1996): 412.

"Come Live With Me." *The Economist*, February 6, 1999, 31.

Coontz, Stephanie. *The Way We Never Were: American Families and the Nostalgia Trap*. New York: Basic Books, 1992.

Crouch, John. Interview on "Time Out" with Jim Parmelee.

DeLaney, Chuck. *Wedding Photography and Video*. New York: Allworth Press, 1994.

Diamant, Anita. *The New Jewish Wedding.* New York: Summit Books, 1985.

Eliade, Marcia, ed. *Encyclopedia of Religion.* New York: Free Press, 1987.

Elwood, Robert S., ed. *Encyclopedia of World Religions.* New York: Book Builders, 1998.

Emrich, Duncan. *The Folklore of Weddings and Marriage.* New York: American Heritage Press, 1970.

Fromm, Erich. *The Art of Loving.* 1956. New York: Harper & Row, 1989.

Gillis, John R. *For Better or Worse: British Marriages, 1600 to the Present.* New York: Oxford University Press, 1985.

Ginsburg, Madeleine. *Wedding Dress, 1740–1970.* London: Her Majesty's Stationery Office, for the Victoria and Albert Museum, 1981.

Goffman, Erving. *Gender Advertisements.* Cambridge: Harvard University Press, 1979.

———. "Hegemony in the Ideal: Wedding Photography, Consumerism, and Patriarchy." *Women's Studies in Communications* 20, no. 2 (Fall 1997): 167–87.

Goldemberg, Rose Leiman. *All about Jewelry: The One Indispensable Guide for Buyers, Wearers, Lovers, Investors.* New York: Arbor House, 1983.

Gottlieb, Beatrice. *The Family in the Western World: From the Black Death to the Industrial Age.* New York and London: Oxford University Press, 1993.

Greeley, Andrew M. *Faithful Attraction: Discovering Intimacy, Love, and Fidelity in American Marriage.* New York: Tor Books, 1991.

Herrick, Robert. "A Ring Presented to Julia." *Poems.* Edited by Ernest Rhys. London: J. M. Dent & Sons, 1936.

Hurth, Robert, and Sheila Hurth. *Wedding Photographer's Handbook.* Amherst, N.Y.: Amherst Media, 1996.

Janus, Samuel S., and Cynthia L. Janus. *The Janus Report on Sexual Behavior.* New York: John Wiley & Sons, 1993.

John Paul II Consortium on Marriage and the Family. "Marriage and Family Fact Sheet." 1999.

Jones, William. *Finger-Ring Lore.* London: Chatto & Windus, 1890.

Kehret, Peg. *Wedding Vows: How to Express Your Love in Your Own Words.* Colorado Springs: Meriwether Publishing, 1989.

Lacey, Peter. *The Wedding.* New York: Grosset & Dunlap, 1969.

Levenstein, Harvey. *Paradox of Plenty: A Social History of Eating in America.* New York: Oxford University Press, 1993.

Lewis, Charles. "Working the Ritual: Professional Wedding Photography and the American Middle Class." *Journal of Communication Inquiry* 22, no. 1 (January 1998): 72–92.

MacClancy, Jeremy. *Consuming Culture: Why You Eat What You Eat*. New York: Henry Holt, 1992.

"Marital Status and Living Arrangements: March 1997 (Update)." Series P-20, n. 506, U.S. Department of Commerce, Census Bureau.

Matlins, Antoinette, Antonio Bonano, and Jane Crystal. *Engagement & Wedding Rings*. South Woodstock, Vt.: Gemstone Press, 1989.

McBride-Mellinger, Maria. *The Wedding Dress*. New York: Random House, 1993.

McCarthy, James Remington. *Rings through the Ages*. New York: Harper & Brothers, 1945.

Milton, John. *The Doctrine and Discipline of Divorce*. In *John Milton: Complete Poetry and Selected Prose*. New York: Modern Library, 1950.

Mordecai, Carolyn. *Weddings: Dating & Love Customs of Cultures Worldwide*. Phoenix: Nittany Publishers, 1999.

Mount, Ferdinand. *The Subversive Family: An Alternative History of Love and Marriage*. New York: Free Press, 1992.

Myers, David G. *The Pursuit of Happiness: Who Is Happy and Why*. New York: William Morrow, 1992.

Nakonezny, Paul A., Robert D. Shull, and Joseph Lee Rodgers. "The Effect of No-Fault Divorce Law on the Divorce Rate Across the 50 States . . ." *Journal of Marriage and the Family* (May 1995): 477–88.

Norfleet, Barbara. *Wedding*. New York: Simon & Schuster, 1979.

Pocs, Ollie. *Our Intimate Relationships: Marriage and the Family*. New York: Harper & Row, 1989.

Popenoe, David, and Barbara Defoe Whitehead. "Should We Live Together? What Young Adults Need to Know about Cohabitation before Marriage." Online publication of The National Marriage Project, Rutgers University, January 1999, 9.

Porter, Roy. *English Society in the Eighteenth Century*. London: Penguin Books, 1990.

Roberts, Sam. *Who We Are: A Portrait of America Based on the Latest U.S. Census*. New York: Random House, 1994.

Rodriguez, Hilda. "Cohabitation: A Snapshot." Factsheet for the Center for Law and Social Policy, May 1998, 5.

Rogers, Jennifer. *Tried and Trousseau: The Bride Guide*. New York: Simon & Schuster, 1992.

Roiphe, Anne. *Generation without Memory: A Jewish Journey in Christian America*. New York: Linden Press/Simon & Schuster, 1981.

Sarett, Morton R. *The Jewelry in Your Life*. Chicago: Nelson-Hall, 1979.

Schaub, George. *Professional Techniques for the Wedding Photographer*. New York: Amphoto, 1985.

Schlessinger, Laura. "The Cohabitation Trap: Your Toothbrushes May Hang Side by Side, But How Together Are You Really?" *Cosmopolitan* 216, no. 3 (March 1994): 92–96H.

Seligson, Marcia. *The Eternal Bliss Machine: America's Way of Wedding*. New York: William Morrow, 1973.

"Should Married Women Take Their Husbands' Name?" *Jet* 92, no. 15 (September 1, 1997).

Sint, Steve. *Wedding Photography: Art, Business, and Style*. Rochester, N.Y.: Silver Pixel Press, 1998.

Stacey, Judith. *In the Name of the Family: Rethinking Family Values in the Postmodern Age*. Boston: Beacon Press, 1996.

Talbot, Margaret. "Love, American Style," *New Republic*, April 14, 1997, 31.

Tasman, Alice Lea Mast. *Wedding Album: Customs and Lore Through the Ages*. New York: Walker & Co., 1982.

Tomasson, Richard F. "Modern Sweden: The Declining Importance of Marriage" *Scandinavian Review*, August 1998.

Tuleja, Tad. *Curious Customs: The Stories Behind 296 Popular American Rituals*. New York: Harmony Books, 1987.

"Unmarried Couple Households." U.S. Bureau of the Census. Internet release date: July 27, 1998.

Visser, Margaret. *The Rituals of Dinner: The Origin, Evolution, Eccentricities, and Meaning of Table Manners*. New York: Grove Press, 1991.

"Vow Wow." *Utne Reader*, May–June 1999, 67.

Credit: Andrew Schotz